Extraordinary People with Disabilities

BY

DEBORAH KENT

KATHRYN A. QUINLAN

Children's Press

A Division of Grolier Publishing

New York London Hong Kong Sydney

Danbury, Connecticut

Acknowledgments

This book could not have been written without the support of many generous and knowledgeable people. Adrienne Asch, Judy Heumann, Deborah Kendrick, Paul Longmore, and Harilyn Rousso made invaluable suggestions regarding people with disabilities whose stories should be part of this collection. Karolyn Koch of the U.S. Paralympic Committee; Abigail Doll of the 1996 Atlanta Paralympic Games; David Phelps of the International Special Olympics; Jerry McCall of USCPAA; and Charley Heubner of USABA shared their thoughts and expertise. Many people at the World Institute on Disability (WID) and the Disability Rights and Education Defense Fund (DREDF) hunted down crucial pieces of information. Deborah Kent would especially like to thank her reader and research assistant, Natalie Conard, for her enthusiasm, efficiency, and endless hours of hard work.

We are especially indebted to the following people, all of whom graciously shared their lives with us through personal interviews: Chris Burke, Beverly Butler, Judi Chamberlin, Jean Driscoll, John Gwaltney, Judy Heumann, Henry Kisor, Susan Nussbaum, Harilyn Rousso, and Hazel (Mrs. Jacobus) tenBroek. To each and every one of these individuals, we offer our heartfelt thanks.

Content Consultant

Stanley D. Klein, Ph.D., Editor in Chief, *Exceptional Parent Magazine: Parenting Your Child with a Disability*

Library of Congress Cataloging-in-Publication Data

Kent, Deborah.
Extraordinary people with disabilities / by Deborah Kent & Kathryn A. Quinlan.
    p. cm. — (Extraordinary people)
Includes bibliographical references and index.
Summary: Profiles several dozen people throughout history with various physical or mental disabilities. Additional articles provide historical background on the disability rights movement.
    ISBN 0-516-20021-6 (lib. bdg.)   ISBN 0-516-26074-X (pbk.)
1. Handicapped—Biography—Juvenile literature. [1. Handicapped.] I. Quinlan, Kathryn A. II. Title.
III. Series.
HV1552.3.K45 1996
363.4'092'2—dc20
[B]
      96-11895
      CIP
      AC

CONTENTS

Introduction **8**

Notes to the Reader **11**

55

FRANKLIN DELANO ROOSEVELT
1882–1945
U.S. President

70

SIR DOUGLAS BADER
1910–1982
Pilot, War Hero

90

BILL VEECK
1914–1986
Baseball Team Owner

59

HORACE PIPPIN
1888–1946
Artist

75

JACOBUS tenBROEK
1911–1968
Educator, Activist

94

ALICIA ALONSO
1921–
Ballet Dancer

63

DOROTHEA LANGE
1895–1965
Photographer

79

HAROLD RUSSELL
1914–
*Actor, Disability Rights
Advocate*

99

ROY CAMPANELLA
1921–1993
Baseball Player

67

FRIDA KAHLO
1907–1954
Artist

83

THE FIGHT FOR
DISABILITY RIGHTS
LEGISLATION

103

ROBERT DOLE
1923–
Politician

159

WILMA MANKILLER
1945–
*Principal Chief of
the Cherokee Nation*

174

FOR THE DISABLED,
OF THE DISABLED

197

JOHN CALLAHAN
1951–
Cartoonist and Activist

163

ITZHAK PERLMAN
1945–
Violinist

181

TEMPLE GRANDIN
1947–
*Livestock-Handling
Equipment Designer*

200

THE RIGHT TO LIVE,
THE RIGHT TO DIE

166

PATTY DUKE
1946–
Actor

186

JUDY HEUMANN
1947–
*Assistant Secretary of
Education*

206

SUSAN NUSSBAUM
1953–
Actor, Playwright

169

HARILYN ROUSSO
1946–
*Disability Rights Activist,
Psychotherapist*

192

STEVIE WONDER
1950–
Musician

209

JOHN HOCKENBERRY
1956–
Journalist

INTRODUCTION

❧

"**W**hat you do is absolutely amazing!" a reporter told a blind ice-skater. "When I think about what you've accomplished, I'm overwhelmed!"

The reporter wasn't talking about the skater's figure eights on the ice. What truly impressed him was the fact that she lived alone, and that her friends raved about her gourmet cooking. "There's nothing remarkable about any of that," the skater pointed out. "I just have a regular life like anybody else."

"But you're so brave," the reporter insisted. "You keep going in spite of your blindness."

"Well," the skater replied, "what are my choices? Would it make more sense for me to sit around and cry?"

In one form or another, people with disabilities have this conversation over and over again throughout their lives. Neighbors, classmates, teachers, and strangers on the street constantly tell them that they are courageous and heroic simply for doing things that most people take for granted. People with disabilities spend endless time and energy trying to prove that they are ordinary people.

A disability is any condition that limits a person's capacity to work, communicate, move, or perform such everyday activities as dressing and cooking. Disabilities may be "obvious" (or observable) conditions, such as blindness, deafness, mental retardation, or paraplegia. Other disabilities may not be so noticeable. Among these "hidden" disabilities are epilepsy, learning disabilities, dyslexia, chronic diseases (AIDS, asthma, arthritis, cancer, diabetes), attention deficit disorder, and mental illnesses such as depression. Some people believe that addiction to drugs or alcohol is a form of disability. So are extreme obesity and facial disfigurement. A person who is very overweight or someone with a scarred face can still work, communicate, move, and perform the activities of daily living. Yet the public perceives that person as being "different." She or he is treated in special ways—ways which society reserves for people with disabilities.

According to United States government figures, about one of every seven Americans has some form of disabling condition. Nearly everyone has at least one relative with a disability—a father with a back problem, a grandmother who uses a hearing aid, a brother with Down syndrome. Since disability is so widespread, one might think people would accept it as an unremarkable fact of life. Instead, disability is regarded by most people as a tragedy. It arouses fear, pity, and sometimes contempt.

For thousands of years, people with disabilities have been seen as hopeless, useless burdens on society. Anything a disabled person managed to do was thought to be a major achievement. This view of disability has been handed down through the ages almost unchanged. People with disabilities are considered to be either helpless or extraordinary.

These two notions seem to be at opposite poles. Actually, however, they both stem from the same bleak picture of life with a disability. When people tell a girl with cerebral palsy that she is astonishing because she baby-sits and has a part in the class play, they are really saying, "I never thought you could do anything worthwhile."

People with disabilities go to school, hold jobs, pursue hobbies, and raise families. Some are generous, some are selfish, some are foolish and some are wise. But most of them spend their lives trying to break down society's stereotypes about who they are. Through their words and actions they try to show the world that they are neither helpless nor outstanding—that, like most people, they fall somewhere between those extremes.

Considering how hard disabled people work to prove that they are regular folks, it seems ironic that this book should be called *Extraordinary People with Disabilities.* The title runs counter to everything disabled people have tried to tell the world about themselves. Yet some people live truly extraordinary lives and make exceptional contributions to society. Some of those extraordinary people are women, and some are men. Some are Caucasian, some are Asian or Latino, and some are of African descent. Some of the world's extraordinary people have disabilities.

The men and women whose stories appear in this book are only a handful of the disabled individuals whose achievements can be ranked as extraordinary. Some of them, such as Franklin D. Roosevelt and Thomas Edison, are familiar to nearly everyone. Others, such as Temple Grandin and Jacobus tenBroek, are well known in highly specialized fields. Some had little contact with other disabled people; some have made the disability rights movement their life's work. Whatever their area of endeavor, the people you will meet in these pages have earned lasting recognition for their accomplishments.

It was Judy Heumann, assistant secretary of education under President Bill Clinton, who put the proper perspective on the title of this book. "As people with disabilities, we've really struggled to be accepted, to blend into society," she commented in an interview. "Now our movement is maturing. We're reaching a point where we can acknowledge that some of us really are exceptional. We shouldn't be afraid to admit that. Every movement has its heroes, and we have ours. It's time for us to celebrate the leaders among us, the people who have made an incredible difference in the world."

So here they are—a sampling of artists and athletes, civil rights activists, scientists, writers, politicians, actors, and scholars. For some, disability has been a major, life-shaping force. For others, it is merely part of the background, overshadowed by a wide range of other experiences. For each of them, disability is one characteristic among many that make up an extraordinary life.

Notes to the Reader

◦——◦

"Sticks and stones can break my bones, but names will never hurt me." On the surface, this familiar phrase makes a lot of sense. But unfortunately, some names can be very hurtful. Other names, however, can be pleasing, attractive, and even empowering.

For decades, people in the disability rights movement have sought to define themselves with empowering words—words free from negative undertones. Disability rights activists dislike demeaning words such as *maimed*, *deformed*, and *crippled*. Many people reject the term *handicapped*, which evokes a sense of pity. To some people *handicapped* sounds like "cap in hand" (as in a beggar on the street). For the most part, people with disabilities believe that terms such as *differently abled*, *physically challenged*, and *handi-capable* are not sincere. These words sound as though they are trying too hard to be positive. The terms disabled and disability are usually preferred. These words are direct and straightforward.

Wherever possible in this book, we use the words *people with disabilities*, rather than *disabled people*. Referring to *people with disabilities* puts the people first. It suggests that the person is more important than whatever disability she or he might have. But repeating the phrase *people with disabilities* too often can lead to long and difficult sentences. In some cases (when *people with disabilities* has already been used in a paragraph), we will use the phrase *disabled people*.

The biographies in this book are arranged chronologically—that is, according to the year in which each person was born. Read in order (from John Milton to Heather Whitestone), they show how society's views on disability have changed over the past three centuries. Most of the people in the early part of this book went through life feeling ashamed of their disabilities. As you will find, much has changed since the 1600s. Civil rights victories are now being won for people with disabilities, and the public's perception of disability in general has shifted away from fear and bigotry.

Interspersed with the biographies in this book are several essays on disability-related topics. These essays give a broader understanding of the disability experience through history and in today's society.

In addition, we have included an extensive "To Find Out More" section at the end of this book. This section includes books, periodicals, Internet sites, and organizations of and for people with disabilities.

JOHN MILTON

1608–1674

Poet

And wisdom at one entrance quite shut out,
So much the rather tho Celestial Light
Shine inward, and though all her powers
Irradiate, there plant eyes, all mist from thence
Purge and dispense, that I may see and tell
Of things invisible to mortal sight.

—*John Milton,* Paradise Lost

The poet John Milton brought light to his own troubled time, and to all the ages since, through some of the most admired poetry ever written in the English language. For the last twenty-two years of his life, he was totally blind. Though grieved by the loss of his sight, John Milton considered his blindness a challenge. He believed that God would replace his sight with a greater vision—the vision of wisdom—and that he could share this illumination with the world through his words.

John Milton was born on December 9, 1608, in a house on Bread Street in London, England. Milton's parents are believed to have been religious Puritans.

They raised their children in a pious, loving home. John had an older sister, Anne, and a younger brother, Christopher, but as the eldest son, John held a special place in his family. His parents were very proud of their first son's cleverness, and they took great care to see that he received a superior education. When he was just seven years old, John began attending St. Paul's, the most respected school in London.

Young John Milton was an eager student. He began writing poetry when he was ten years old and rarely left his studies before midnight. Milton's father encouraged him in his study of poetry and the humanities. At sixteen, John entered Christ's College at Cambridge University, where he decided that he would study to enter the ministry. Despite this decision, he continued to write poetry throughout his years at Cambridge. In 1628, he composed a poem to comfort his sister following the death of her infant child and, in 1629, he wrote an ode entitled "On the Morning of Christ's Nativity."

John Milton graduated from Cambridge in March 1629 and decided to remain in school to pursue his master's degree. When he attained this degree in 1632, Milton left Cambridge and moved to one of his father's houses in Horton, Buckinghamshire, near London. Milton remained at Horton for three years, reading, studying, and writing poetry.

During the quiet years at Horton, John Milton realized that he was not destined to enter the ministry. In 1633, King Charles I appointed William Laud as the Archbishop of Canterbury. Laud forced the clergy throughout England to conform to rigid ritual. Milton realized that he needed greater freedom of thought than was possible for clergy under the reign of King Charles I and Archbishop Laud. He remained determined to serve God, but he intended to do so through his poetry.

In the following years, Milton produced two works that are notable as his first great efforts. The first, *Comus*, was a "masque," or a brief play with some musical pieces. The second, *Lycidas*, was written in memory of a college friend who died tragically by drowning. This type of poem is called a eulogy. To this day, *Lycidas* is considered by many experts to be the greatest eulogy ever written.

In 1638, John left England to travel throughout continental Europe. He visited some of the world's most beautiful cities, including Paris, Florence, Rome, and Naples. In each city, Milton met great scholars, poets, and political thinkers. This was one of the happiest times in his life. Milton ended his travels abruptly, however, when he learned of approaching civil war in his native England. He felt that he could not remain abroad while people struggled for freedom at home.

In 1639, England was torn by religious and political controversy. Some citizens thought that all people should conform to the same beliefs and rituals. Many of these people considered the king an absolute monarch, one with the right to govern the practices of both the state and the church. Others in England believed that people should be free to choose their own faith and that kings should answer to the nation's people. These opposing groups fought bitterly.

Milton became involved in these struggles and wrote political pamphlets that sparked passionate debate throughout England. He believed strongly in religious freedom and felt that rulers must be accountable to the nations they govern. Those who shared Milton's beliefs thought him a champion of their cause. The Royalists, who believed in the absolute rule of kings, were outraged by Milton's ideas.

By 1642, the conflict had moved beyond words, and the country erupted in civil war. In 1649, King Charles I was removed from the throne, put on trial as a tyrant, and executed. A new government was formed, founded on democratic principles. The government was led by a man named Oliver Cromwell. This period in England's history is called the Reformation.

Milton supported Oliver Cromwell and served in several literary posts within Cromwell's government. He wrote numerous pamphlets explaining and defending decisions made by Cromwell's government. During these years, Milton's sight began to fail. By 1652, at age forty-four, he was completely blind.

In Milton's time, doctors understood very little about diseases of the eye. Many people regarded blindness as a punishment from God. Milton's Royalist foes claimed that he was being punished for arguing against the king. Milton believed that his blindness was a sign of God's favor. He felt that God was testing him, as the faithful in the Old Testament had been tested, in order to make him stronger.

The Reformation lasted only a few short years. In 1660, Royalists brought King Charles II to rule, in a movement that is now called the Restoration. After the Restoration, many of those who had supported Cromwell were exiled or put to death. Milton was in danger, but he was spared, in part, because of his blindness. He did not suffer punishment under Charles II, but he did lose his primary source of income and all the money he had invested in the Reformation government. He soon became a relatively poor man.

After the Restoration, Milton retired from political life to focus on his writing. With assistance from friends who put his words on paper for him, Milton began writing the great work of his life, *Paradise Lost.* This work is a tremendous epic poem about the fall of Adam and Eve from the Garden of Eden. Milton followed this epic with another, shorter epic poem, called *Paradise Regained.* During this period of his life, Milton also produced a history of Britain.

In Milton's time, few blind people had the chance to lead full, productive lives. Most people expected blind persons to be of little use in the world. After the loss of his sight, Milton himself sometimes doubted his own value. In a poem called *On His Blindness,* he asks, "Doth God exact day-labor, light denied?" After reflecting that God had thousands of servants to "speed and post o'er land and ocean without rest," he concluded, "They also serve who only stand and wait." In this poem, Milton seems to deny the worth of his achievements, and to say that as a blind man he can do nothing but wait passively.

John Milton died on November 8, 1674. During his lifetime, he fought for religious freedom and for the principles of democracy. He died before these causes would succeed. But he left behind an enduring body of poetry that has inspired countless readers to continue in their faith and in their struggle for freedom. Through his words, John Milton has been a source of great light for those who believe in freedom of religious expression and democracy, and for those who love poetry. His wisdom enabled him to "see and tell of things invisible to mortal sight."

1770–1827

Composer

Ludwig van Beethoven was born into a family of musicians. His grandfather, for whom he was named, was a highly praised bass singer, and his father, Johann Beethoven, was a court tenor and music teacher. From his earliest years, young Ludwig knew that he, too, would pursue a life in music. He began learning to play the piano when he was only four years old.

Beethoven grew up in Bonn, Germany, in a home filled with tension. His mother, Maria Magdalena, was gentle and loving, but she was very unhappy in her marriage. Ludwig's father never equaled his own father's success as a musician. To combat his sense of failure, Johann Beethoven pushed young Ludwig without mercy. Sometimes he woke the boy at midnight and forced him to practice playing the piano until dawn. Johann Beethoven wanted his son to become a child prodigy like the famous Wolfgang Amadeus Mozart. Though Ludwig was an exceptionally talented pianist, he did not reveal his true genius until he reached adulthood.

Early in Ludwig's childhood, Johann Beethoven began drinking heavily. As he lapsed into alcoholism, he could no longer work. When Ludwig was eleven, he left school and helped support his mother and five younger brothers and sisters by working as a court musician. At fourteen, the boy became a deputy court organist.

During these years, Beethoven worked under Christian Gottlob Neefe, a German composer, organist, and conductor. Neefe recognized his young assistant's talent and instructed him in both performance and composing. Beethoven admired Neefe both as a musician and as a man of integrity. Under Neefe's guidance, Beethoven's musical ability improved and eventually surpassed his father's.

In 1787, at the age of seventeen, Beethoven prepared for a journey to Vienna, Austria, where he was to play for the great Mozart. But before he could depart, he received a frantic message from his father. His mother was very ill. Beethoven rushed home to Bonn to be with her when she died of tuberculosis. Since Johann Beethoven could not care for his family, Ludwig became the breadwinner. For the next four years, he shouldered his family responsibilities. He fulfilled his duties as a court musician, and he worked as a music teacher to add to his family's income.

Beethoven's life changed dramatically in 1792, when the world-renowned musician Franz Joseph Haydn accepted him as a student. Early in November, Ludwig van Beethoven set out for Vienna to study with the celebrated master. He never saw his birthplace again.

Haydn was not a patient teacher, and his relationship with Beethoven was always stormy. Nevertheless, Beethoven applied himself to learning the rules of music composition. Until this time, he was known chiefly as a virtuoso pianist. Now he began to make his mark as a composer as well. Soon his reputation swept across Europe. He wrote sonatas (pieces for solo instruments) and concertos (pieces for solo instruments accompanied by orchestra). Beethoven's most striking compositions were his symphonies—long works in which the orchestra showed its full range of expression.

In the late 1700s and early 1800s, musicians depended on a system of patronage for their survival. Members of the nobility became a musician's patrons, providing money for support. Beethoven quickly gained a number of wealthy admirers who were willing to give him sums of money. But he did not get along well in social situations. He was gruff and outspoken, and he was easily offended by others. His relationships with patrons were marred by frequent quarrels. Despite his difficult temperament, however, Ludwig van Beethoven won many supporters who remained loyal throughout his lifetime.

In 1802, Beethoven wrote a letter to his two brothers. He explained that ill health was the cause for his behavior. He wrote, "For six years I have been in a hopeless case, made worse by ignorant doctors, yearly betrayed in the hope of getting better, finally forced to face the prospect of a permanent malady. . . ." Beethoven was in a state of crisis. He knew that he was gradually becoming deaf.

For a man whose life revolved around music, the realization of losing his sense of hearing must have been devastating. Beethoven became increasingly irritable and morose. He could no longer perform with the subtlety and beauty that had once made him famous. The great composer could not hear his own compositions. At times Beethoven sank into despair. Yet he wrote defiantly to a friend, "I will seize fate by the throat!"

Though Beethoven could no longer hear chords and melodies, music was still alive in his mind. Even as his hearing faded, his compositions became more original. Beethoven moved beyond the typical musical styles of his day and created a stirring, emotional, and heroic composing style. Today he is recognized for teaching the world to value instrumental music as highly as music for voices. Beethoven's nine completed symphonies are now ranked among the greatest in classical music.

By 1819, Ludwig van Beethoven was profoundly deaf. Wherever he went, he carried a "conversation book," a notebook in which friends wrote questions and comments. Beethoven read their words and answered aloud. His greatest work, the magnificent Ninth Symphony, was completed in 1824. During the work's first performance, Beethoven sat on the stage, reading the score. After the glorious final movement, the audience burst into applause. But Beethoven could not hear them. One of the musicians touched his shoulder and urged him to face the audience. He saw hundreds of people on their feet, clapping and cheering. Beethoven knew how powerfully his music had touched them.

Beethoven continued to compose music until his death from pneumonia on March 26, 1827. More than twenty thousand people attended his funeral. Today Beethoven is revered as one of the finest composers the world has ever known.

THADDEUS STEVENS

1792–1868

U.S. Congressman

I n 1792, less than ten years after the end of the Revolutionary War, Vermont lay at the edge of the western frontier in North America. Its untamed forests and stony soil were a trial to the hardiest farmer. When Thaddeus Stevens was born near the village of Danville, Vermont, his mother was afraid for his future. In those days, only the physically strong had a chance to survive. Her youngest son, Thaddeus, was born with a clubfoot, a condition in which one foot is turned inward, making it difficult to walk. Today this condition can be corrected with surgery and special shoes.

Thaddeus Stevens was the youngest of four boys. His father, a shoemaker, disappeared when Thaddeus was small, and the boy grew up in desperate poverty. Yet his mother was determined that he should receive an education. Because of his disability, she was convinced that he could not become a farmer like his older brothers. She believed that education was his only hope.

Thaddeus's mother filled him with ambition. She told him that he could become a minister, one of the most respected members of the community. At the same time, she felt that he would always be isolated because of his clubfoot. She did not believe that any woman would want to marry a man who walked with a limp. Thaddeus Stevens grew up with a fierce determination to succeed in a profession, but he had little confidence in his ability to make friends.

Other boys often teased Thaddeus because he spent so much time with his mother and rarely took part in rough-and-tumble games. Years later one acquaintance remembered that Thaddeus was "still and quiet . . . different from the rest of the boys, who would laugh at him . . . and mimic his limping walk." Thaddeus was deeply sensitive, and his feelings were easily hurt.

To obtain an education for Thaddeus, Mrs. Stevens moved the family to the town of Peacham, Vermont. There Thaddeus entered Peacham Academy. Thaddeus thrived in an atmosphere where Latin and philosophy were more important than anything else. For the first time in his life, he felt that he was equal to the people around him. He saw that education was an essential tool for the creation of a true democracy.

In 1811, Thaddeus Stevens entered Dartmouth College. He was known as a headstrong student who often ran into conflict with his teachers. But he was an eloquent speaker, recognized for his clear thinking and his ability to put ideas into words.

Despite his mother's urging, Stevens had no interest in the ministry. After graduating from Dartmouth, he taught at a boys' school in York, Pennsylvania. He also studied law on his own, using books he borrowed from a friend. In 1816, he passed the bar examination in Maryland and opened a law practice in the Pennsylvania town of Gettysburg. At first, he had few clients and plenty of leisure time for reading. Then, in 1821, Stevens won an important murder case by pleading his client's insanity. His reputation spread rapidly, and soon clients flocked to his office. Stevens's powerful oral arguments won case after case before the Pennsylvania Supreme Court.

In the years when Stevens was building his law practice, Pennsylvania was a staunch "free state" where slavery was forbidden. But in neighboring Maryland, many people owned slaves. Frequently runaway slaves fled from Maryland into Pennsylvania seeking freedom. Thaddeus Stevens defended many such fugitives in court, taking their cases free of charge. The more he saw of slavery, the more Stevens grew to despise it.

Throughout his life, Stevens had a deep sympathy for all oppressed people. Yet he was a lonely man. He never married and had few close friends. He seemed to live out his mother's prediction that he would be a success in his chosen profession but a social outcast.

In 1826, Stevens launched a business venture, an ironworks near Chambersburg, Pennsylvania. At first, he and his partner, James Paxton, manufactured iron stoves. Later they opened the Caledonian Forge, where pig iron was mixed with other ores to produce stronger alloys. The business was never very profitable. As time passed, Stevens kept the forge running to provide jobs for people in the community.

Stevens's interest in community affairs was growing. In 1833, he was elected to the Pennsylvania House of Representatives, where he served until 1841. He strongly supported an 1834 measure that established free public schools throughout the state. The following year, the new school system was threatened when citizens protested a rise in state taxes. Stevens fought back, delivering a brilliant speech in defense of education and the principles of democracy. The repeal of free education, he insisted, would be "an act for branding and marking the poor." The House and the Senate gave way to Stevens's arguments, and the public schools were saved.

In 1842, Stevens returned to the practice of law. For several years he worked to pay back debts that had accumulated from his struggling iron business. He had not lost his interest in politics, and in 1848, he ran for Congress. He was elected as a member of the Whig Party and set off for a new life in Washington.

As a U.S. congressman, Stevens threw himself into the fight against slavery. In passionate speeches he denounced slavery as "a curse, a shame, and a crime." He fiercely opposed every attempt to extend it into U.S. territories that had not yet become states. His hatred of slavery overflowed to the Southern people who kept it alive. He called them "slave-drivers" and accused them of crimes against humanity. On the slavery issue, Stevens refused to accept any compromise.

Few other Whigs were willing to take Stevens's unyielding stand. Frustrated by his party's moderation, Stevens left Congress in 1853. Three years later, he took a leading role in the formation of the antislavery Republican Party. In 1856, he spoke in Philadelphia at the nation's first Republican National Convention. One member of the audience later wrote that he "never heard a man speak with more feeling or in more persuasive accents."

Stevens returned to Congress as a Republican in 1858. By then, tensions between the North and South were near the breaking point. Stevens continued to push for the unconditional abolition of slavery. When some of the Southern states threatened to secede from the Union, Stevens warned, "Our next United States will contain no foot of ground on which a slave can tread, no breath of air which a slave can breathe."

Most Southerners were appalled when Abraham Lincoln was elected president in 1860. But Stevens gave only reluctant support to Lincoln. Lincoln, too, opposed slavery and did not want it to extend into the territories, but he had no plans to forbid the practice in the states where it already existed. To Thaddeus Stevens, Lincoln was a weak moderate, willing to sacrifice principles for convenience.

When the nation erupted into civil war, Stevens headed the powerful House Ways and Means Committee. The committee was responsible for raising much of the money needed for the military. Stevens devised ingenious methods of raising funds through taxes. Though he and Lincoln still had serious differences, Stevens gave the president his full support when it came to the war effort.

In 1864, Southern troops swept into Chambersburg, destroying the Caledonian Forge. In a letter Stevens described how the enemy "took all my horses, mules, and harness . . . seized bacon, molasses, and grain, burned the furnace, rolling mill, and forges. . . . They even hauled off my bar iron, [it] being, as they said, convenient for shoeing horses, about $4000 worth." With the forge gone, Stevens provided for the stricken families of his workers.

When peace came at last, Lincoln hoped to rebuild the beaten South, bringing it back into the Union as smoothly as possible. After Lincoln's assassination, President Andrew Johnson tried to carry out the reconstruction programs that the deceased president had planned. Stevens believed the reconstruction program was too lenient. He wanted the South to be punished, treated as "a conquered province." He also was determined that African-Americans should be granted their full civil rights. To his grief, the civil rights measures he supported were weakened drastically before they passed. Thaddeus Stevens became President Johnson's enemy. In 1866 and again in 1867, Stevens supported resolutions in Congress for Johnson's impeachment. The 1867 resolution failed to pass by only one vote.

Already in failing health, Stevens was crushed when the impeachment resolution was defeated. When Congress recessed, he was too ill to return to Pennsylvania. He died in Washington, with his nephew and his housekeeper at his bedside. Stevens was buried in Lancaster, Pennsylvania. His tombstone bears an inscription that he wrote: "I repose in this quiet, secluded spot, not from any natural preference for solitude; but finding other cemeteries limited by character rules as to race, I have chosen this, that I might illustrate in my death the principles which I advocated through a long life: the equality of man before his creator."

LOUIS BRAILLE

1809–1852

Creator of a Reading System for the Blind

In the early 1800s, most blind individuals were condemned to lives of poverty and ignorance. Few schools existed for blind children, and those that did could teach only the most basic skills. They had no practical way to teach the blind to read. Many blind individuals were forced to roam the streets, begging for food. Others were cast into institutions for the mentally ill. The most fortunate could look forward only to depending on others for the rest of their lives.

In 1824, a fifteen-year-old boy named Louis Braille gave blind people the key to independence. Using a system of raised dot patterns that could be "seen" by fingertips rather than eyes, he created a new system of reading. Braille's system could be read and written very quickly. Blind people could learn to read and write. Today, Louis Braille's system of reading is used by sightless individuals the world over. We call the system "Braille," after its inventor.

Louis Braille was born on January 4, 1809, in Coupvray, a small French village 20 miles (32 kilometers) east of Paris. The youngest child of Simon Rene and Monique Braille, Louis was a bright, curious little boy. Simon Rene was fond of predicting that the boy would grow up to be a professor, but Louis could imagine nothing better than becoming a harness maker like his father. Louis loved to visit his father in the harness shop. His father let him play with the soft, pleasant-smelling scraps of leather. Louis would imagine that the scraps were soldiers from Napoleon's army, or he'd pretend to make elegant saddles and harnesses like those his father made.

One day, while his father was occupied with a customer, three-year-old Louis grew tired of pretending. He was eager to begin using his father's bright tools to make real harnesses. Standing on the tips of his toes, Louis reached for the awl—a long, pointed tool used to punch holes in leather. He tried to bring the awl down upon the leather as he had seen his father do, but his small hand lost its grip on the tool. The awl slipped, piercing his left eye. In the days that followed, Louis's parents and the village doctor did all they could to save his vision. But medicine in the 1800s was very primitive, and the injured eye soon became infected. The infection quickly spread to Louis's other eye, and he became completely blind.

At first, Louis was bewildered by the change. He no longer could run freely about his house and farm. He felt lost and frightened in the dark. The Braille family encouraged Louis to be as independent as possible. His father made him a small cane so that he could feel his way around as he walked. In time, Louis learned to move about his home and the town without assistance.

As Louis grew, he yearned to play games and attend school with the other village children. Recognizing the boy's intelligence, the town priest, Father Jacques Palluy, began teaching him at the church. Louis eagerly absorbed the poetry, history, and biblical stories that Father Palluy shared with him. The priest was impressed by the boy's abilities and urged the local schoolmaster to allow Louis to attend school with the other children. The teacher was doubtful that Louis would succeed, but agreed to let him try. Louis was thrilled. He listened attentively to all of the lessons and asked other children to read the schoolbooks aloud to him.

When Louis Braille was ten years old, Father Palluy learned of a school for blind boys in Paris. At that school, the boys were taught to play musical instruments, and they learned useful skills that would enable them to support themselves in adulthood. Best of all, the school had special books made with raised letters that blind people could feel with their hands. At last, Louis would be able to read!

On February 15, 1819, Louis entered the National Institute for Blind Youth. At first, the school seemed strange to the young boy from the country. It was large and damp, and many of the boys were rough and unruly. Louis was the youngest of sixty students. As he made friends, however, he began to enjoy life at the school. He learned geography, history, and music. He also made slippers and knitted caps that were sold throughout Paris.

After several months at the school, Louis asked a teacher when he would learn to read. The teacher explained that the school had only three books for blind readers. Because the books were made with large, raised print, they were very expensive and difficult to make. Louis was bitterly disappointed. He had hoped for an entire library of books.

Louis's disappointment increased when he began reading the school's few books. The raised print was difficult for a blind person to understand because the letters had so many lines and curves. Louis soon realized that the raised letters were not a practical way for blind people to read. He became determined to create a reading system for blind people. He wanted to be able to read a printed page as quickly and easily as a sighted person.

During the next few years, Louis struggled to create his reading system. When Louis was twelve, a French army captain named Charles Barbier visited the school. Captain Barbier had invented a system that allowed soldiers to send silent messages in the dark. He called it "night writing." Night writing used raised dots and dashes to represent sounds. By feeling the pattern of dots poked through heavy paper, soldiers could read messages in the dark. The system had many flaws and could be used only for very simple messages, but Louis was inspired.

Over the next three years, Louis worked to adapt Barbier's code to an alphabet for the blind. He eliminated the dashes and created a "cell" consisting of six dots that could fit easily beneath a blind person's fingertip. The cell was three lines deep and two lines wide: 1 4

2 5

3 6

Within the cell, Louis raised patterns of dots to represent different letters, as follows:

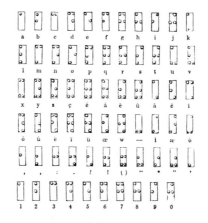

At age fifteen, Louis Braille succeeded where all others had failed. He created a system of reading and writing that made information accessible to the blind. The students at the National Institute for Blind Youth quickly recognized the value of Louis's reading system and were eager to begin using it.

At seventeen, Braille became an instructor at the National Institute for Blind Youth, where he remained until his death in 1852. Throughout his adulthood, Louis struggled to promote the use of Braille. Today, the Braille system is used by blind individuals throughout the world. Louis Braille's dream of libraries filled with books for the blind has become a reality.

HARRIET TUBMAN

c. 1820–1913

Rescuer of Slaves

The girl called Araminta swept floors, cared for babies, and scrubbed pots and pans in the kitchen. She was busy from morning until night, but her master complained that she was not a good worker. She had a rebellious streak—not a desirable trait in a slave.

Araminta was born on a plantation in Dorchester County on Maryland's eastern shore. Both of her grandparents had been born in Africa and brought as slaves to the New World. When she grew older, Araminta took her mother's name, Harriet.

One day, when Harriet was thirteen years old, she saw the plantation overseer preparing to whip a fellow slave. Harriet threw herself between them, and the overseer struck her on the head with a 2-pound (0.9-kilogram) weight. She fell unconscious, her skull fractured by the blow.

Harriet recovered slowly. For the rest of her life she had a form of epilepsy, a seizure disorder. From time to time, with little warning, she would sink into a sleeplike state from which she could not be awakened.

During her long recovery from her injury, Harriet had a lot of time to think. Years later she told a friend, "As I lay so sick on my bed from Christmas till March, I was always praying for poor old Master. 'Oh dear Lord, change that man's heart and make him a Christian!'" Her master, however, showed no sign of mending his ways. When Harriet learned that she and one of her brothers were to be sold to work on a chain gang in the Deep South, she changed her prayer. "Lord," she prayed, "if you ain't never going to change the man's heart, kill him, Lord, and take him out of the way so he won't do no more mischief!" This time, her prayer was answered. Her master died unexpectedly. Harriet was not sold. Awed by a sense of power, she prayed that the Lord would "cleanse my soul of sin."

For several years after Harriet's injury, she and her father were sent to work in a nearby lumberyard. Harriet grew extremely strong with all of the hard physical labor. The work at the mill also enabled her to earn a bit of money for her own use.

When she was twenty-four years old, Harriet married a free black man named John Tubman. The following year, she learned that her mother had once been granted her freedom in the will of a former master. Because her mother could not read or write, and had no knowledge of her rights under the law, the will was overturned and she remained a slave. Harriet was stunned by this discovery. If her mother had been freed, then Harriet and her brothers and sisters would all have grown up in freedom.

In 1849, Harriet Tubman again heard rumors that she was to be sold. This time she decided to escape. Though she was in constant danger of capture, she managed to reach Philadelphia, where slavery was not permitted. She worked at a hotel, saving money and making secret plans.

After several months in Philadelphia, Harriet Tubman slipped back into Maryland. She contacted one of her sisters and helped her escape with her two children. In 1851, she rescued her brother and his family. Soon afterward, she led a daring escape involving eleven people.

No one knows for certain how many slaves Harriet Tubman led to freedom during the next ten years. Some historians believe she helped as many as three hundred people. She worked as part of the Underground Railroad, a secret network of black and white abolitionists who aided fugitive slaves on their journeys. Slaves were hidden in wagons under loads of hay and sheltered in "safe houses" until they could move on.

While slaveholders tried to hunt her down, Harriet Tubman was a hero to abolitionists (people who wanted to end, or abolish, slavery). She frequently spoke at antislavery conventions, telling her own story and describing the lives of slaves she had rescued. "Harriet was a woman of no pretensions," wrote the abolitionist leader William Still, himself a former slave. "Indeed, a more ordinary specimen of humanity could hardly be found among the most unfortunate-looking farmhands of the south. Yet, in point of courage, shrewdness, and disinterested exertion to rescue her fellow men by making personal visits into Maryland among the slaves, she was without her equal."

Harriet Tubman believed that her work was inspired and guided by divine powers. She felt that God spoke to her through dreams and omens. When the Civil War broke out in 1861, she was not at all surprised. She had already seen the terrible conflict in a vision. In 1862, Tubman made her way through the war-torn South to South Carolina and offered her services to the Union army. For the next three years, she worked as a scout and spy. Slaves often overheard bits of information as they waited on tables or polished their masters' boots. They passed each tidbit to Harriet Tubman, who relayed it to Union headquarters.

In the years after the Civil War, Harriet Tubman settled in Auburn, New York, to care for her aged parents. Eventually she took in several more elderly black people who were in need of help. With the aid of friends, she founded the Harriet Tubman Home for Indigent Aged Negroes, which operated well into the twentieth century. Tubman also promoted the establishment of "freedman's schools," where former slaves were taught to read and write. Though she was illiterate all her life, she had tremendous respect for education.

Harriet Tubman believed fervently that all people—black and white, man and woman—must work together as equals. In the late nineteenth century, as women began the long struggle for equal rights, she heard echoes of the fight she had helped to wage against slavery. She became a staunch supporter of Susan B. Anthony in her crusade for women's suffrage. Once a reporter asked her if women should have the right to vote. "Yes," she replied, "I have suffered enough in life to believe it."

John Wesley Powell

1834–1902

Explorer, Geologist

In the middle of the nineteenth century, when John Wesley Powell was growing up, countless people traveled to the American West, which they saw as an unexplored frontier. "Wes," as he was known to his family, was born in New York State. But his father, a traveling Methodist preacher, soon led the family into the wild lands to the west. The Powells moved to Ohio, then headed farther west to Wisconsin, then finally put down roots on the prairies of Illinois.

Wes's father urged his son to follow him into the ministry, but Wes had no desire to become a preacher. He was fascinated by rocks, birds, and trees, and he loved to search the woods for Indian arrowheads. When he announced his plans to study natural history in college, his father refused to pay his tuition.

In 1861, the United States was torn by civil war. Powell enlisted with the Union army, where he rose to the rank of major. He was wounded at the Battle of Shiloh in 1862 and lost his right arm below the elbow. When Powell returned to civilian life, his father was convinced that Wes's disability would put a halt to his earlier plans. Now, at last, he would accept the life of a minister. "Wes, you are a maimed man," he told his son. "Get this notion of science and adventure out of your mind."

But John Wesley Powell had lost none of his old enthusiasm for the outdoors. He found a supporter in his cousin, Emma Beam, who eventually became his wife. Together they hiked, climbed mountains, and rowed through streams and rivers.

In 1865, Powell became a professor of natural science at Illinois Wesleyan University. The position gave him ample opportunity to conduct exploring and collecting expeditions into the little-known region west of the Mississippi. In 1867, he led a group of students on a trip through the Rocky Mountains. During this trip, he conceived the idea of an expedition down the Colorado River through the heart of the Grand Canyon.

More than three centuries before, the Spanish explorer Francisco Coronado became the first European to glimpse the magnificent canyon created by the Colorado River. But by the 1860s, the canyon's rocky walls and churning rapids were known only to American Indians and a few white trappers. The Grand Canyon never had been explored completely, from end to end.

For the next two years, Powell planned his trip down the Colorado. He raised enough money to equip a ten-month expedition. With the help of a Chicago boatyard, he designed four sturdy craft with watertight compartments to hold food supplies and scientific instruments. At last, in May 1869, the expedition set out down the Green River, a branch of the mighty Colorado River in Wyoming Territory. Powell was accompanied by his brother, Walter; a teenage mule driver; an English adventurer; an army sergeant named George Y. Bradley; and five trappers.

Almost from the start, the expedition ran into trouble. After barely two weeks on the river, one of the boats struck a rock. The bottom split, spilling one-third of Powell's precious supplies into the water. In the weeks that followed, the men complained more and more bitterly about the scarce food, the mosquitoes, and having to travel overland when river rapids blocked their way. The crew sneered at Powell's interest in rocks and often challenged his authority.

Despite these troubles, Powell was dazzled by the beauty of the Grand Canyon. "A year scarcely suffices to see it all," he wrote later. "You cannot see the Grand Canyon in one view, as if it were a changeless spectacle from which a curtain might be lifted. To see it, you have to toil from month to month through its labyrinth."

One morning, Powell and Bradley set out on a scouting expedition. Near the top of a 100-foot (30-meter) precipice, Powell became stranded. He had a firm foothold, and he gripped an outcropping of rock with his hand. But he could go no farther, either up or down. Bradley climbed to a place above him but could not reach Powell to help him. "The moment was critical," Powell wrote later. "Standing on my toes, my muscles began to tremble. . . . If I lost my hold, I would fall to the bottom." Then Bradley had a brilliant idea. He yanked off his trousers and swung them within Powell's reach. Powell "hugged close to the rocks, let go with my hand, seized the dangling legs, and with his assistance I was enabled to gain the top."

On the expedition's ninety-sixth day, Powell and his men encountered yet another set of rapids. These looked worse than any they had seen before. The canyon walls were so steep that a portage would be impossible. Somehow they would have to shoot the rapids in their fragile wooden boats.

Suddenly three of the trappers rebelled, declaring that they would go no farther. Powell feared that the whole expedition had come to an end. The thought was devastating. In his diary he wrote, "To leave the exploration unfinished, to say that there is a part of the canyon which I cannot explore, having almost accomplished it, is more than I am willing to acknowledge."

The three rebellious trappers did abandon the expedition. They climbed the perilous canyon walls of the north rim, only to be killed by American Indians. Powell and the remaining explorers successfully navigated the rapids and emerged from the Grand Canyon on August 29, 1869. "Now the danger is over, now the toil has ceased," Powell wrote. "The river rolls by us in silent majesty. The quiet of the camp is sweet. Our joy is almost ecstasy."

Powell's triumph made headlines all over the country. Overnight he became a celebrity. He toured the land, delivering lectures about his experiences and his theories on geology. Now that he was famous, Powell was able to arouse interest in some of the projects he held most dear. He was thrilled when Congress gave him ten thousand dollars to launch a geographic and geological survey of the whole Rocky Mountain region. For the first time, the vast lands of the West could be studied by scientists.

In 1871, Powell led a second expedition down the Green and Colorado Rivers. For the next nine years, he lived in Utah Territory, studying the region's unique geology. He also developed an intense interest in American Indian cultures. He learned to speak two Indian languages fluently—Ute and Southern Paiute. For several months, he lived with the Kaibab Paiute on the north rim of the Grand Canyon, gathering information about their language, music, and customs.

Powell was keenly aware that Indian cultures were fast disappearing under increasing white settlement. In 1879, he founded the Smithsonian Institution's Bureau of Ethnology to study and record the traditions of Native American people. He directed the bureau for the next twenty-three years.

After decades of service in government, Powell spent his final years with his wife in a cottage on the Maine coast. He wrote philosophical essays, took friends on nature walks, and reminisced about his rugged days in the West.

Powell's ideas were not forgotten. Only a few months after his death, President Theodore Roosevelt asked Congress to establish a federal program for planning irrigation projects in the West. Roosevelt's program evolved into the Bureau of Reclamation, which still operates today. "If we could save the water running to waste," Roosevelt declared, "the western part of the country could sustain a population greater than even legendary Major Powell dreamed."

THOMAS EDISON

$\backsim$

1834–1931

Inventor

I n 1847, people read at night by the light of candles or lanterns. If they wanted music, they had to make their own by singing or playing an instrument. And nobody had ever heard of going to a movie on a Saturday night. The electric light, the phonograph, and the motion-picture projector all sprang from the creative genius of a single man—Thomas Alva Edison. But few people realize that from childhood, Thomas Edison had severely impaired hearing.

Thomas Edison was born on February 11, 1847, in Milan, Ohio, the seventh and last child of Samuel and Nancy Edison. From the beginning, Tom was intrigued by the way things worked. His parents called him the "nervous little question box." His curiosity sometimes led Tom into misadventures. When he was four years old, he nearly drowned while exploring the workings of a shipyard.

In 1854, the Edison family moved to Port Huron, Michigan, where Tom spent the rest of his youth. Shortly after the move, Tom caught scarlet fever. The illness permanently damaged the hearing in both of his ears and left him too weak and frail to begin school until he was over eight years old. His experience in the classroom was discouraging. The teacher, Mr. Engle, expected his students to memorize their lessons quietly. He found Tom's constant questions and nonstop activity very disruptive. Some experts today suspect that Thomas Edison had attention deficit disorder (ADD), a form of learning disability that causes hyperactivity and a short attention span. Clearly, as can be seen in Edison's case, ADD does not limit a person's intelligence.

After Tom had struggled at school for three months, his mother decided to teach him at home. Because he was such an eager reader, she knew he could learn without going to school. Through extensive reading, Tom began to learn about electricity. He decided that he was going to become an inventor and immediately began conducting experiments. By the time he was twelve, he needed to earn money for equipment and supplies. He found work selling candy, sandwiches, and newspapers on a train of the Grand Trunk Railway. The train left Port Huron at 7:00 A.M. and did not return until 9:30 P.M. Tom even began publishing his own newspaper, the *Weekly Herald*, which he sold to passengers on the train.

One morning, Tom arrived for work just as the train was pulling out of the station. He ran after the train and a friendly conductor grabbed him by the head to pull him aboard. Tom felt something pop in his ears. The conductor had accidentally done further harm to his already limited hearing.

Tom worked on the train for three years. He made friends with many of the telegraph operators along the train line. One friend was J. U. MacKenzie. Tom loved to watch MacKenzie operate the train's telegraph machine. He longed to learn the code so that he, too, could become a telegraph operator. One day, when Tom was fifteen years old, he saw Mackenzie's young son, Jimmy, standing on the railroad tracks as a boxcar was rushing toward him. He raced to save the boy and snatched him out of the boxcar's path just in time. MacKenzie was so grateful that he offered to teach Tom how to operate the telegraph. Tom learned quickly. By the time he was sixteen, he was a fully qualified telegraph operator. For the next five years, he wandered from town to town, supporting himself by working as a telegrapher.

When Thomas Edison was twenty-one, he moved to New York City, where he found work fixing and improving machines used in large factories. He continued to work on inventions, and he secured his first patent, for a vote-counting machine. While living in New York, Edison met and married a quiet, gentle young woman named Mary Stilwell.

In 1870, Edison completed his first commercially successful invention, a more efficient ticker-tape machine for the stock market. He earned a small fortune by manufacturing his Edison Universal Stock Printer in Newark, New Jersey.

At age twenty-nine, Thomas Edison had saved enough money to begin pursuing his dreams. He and Mary moved to Menlo Park, New Jersey, where he built an "invention factory." With a crew of clockmakers, mechanics, and mathematicians, he worked tirelessly to turn his ideas into realities. One of his projects was a machine that could "talk." In 1877, Edison developed the phonograph, a machine that could reproduce sounds, speech, and music.

Soon after inventing the phonograph, Edison began his search for a cheap, reliable way of lighting homes and businesses. In those days, people used gas-fueled lights, which were expensive and sometimes dangerous. Many people had tried unsuccessfully to create an electric light that would burn steadily without going out. Edison's initial efforts were not promising. He ran electricity through two metal wires and a carbon filament. The gadget gave off light for a moment, but quickly became too hot and burned the filament. Edison pondered the problem for several months. In 1879, Edison discovered that air caused the light to become too hot and burn out. By putting the wires and filament in an airless vacuum, he created an electric light that burned for forty continuous hours. The nation hailed Thomas Edison as the inventor of the electric light bulb.

By now, Edison was wealthy and famous. Yet his personal life was marred with sorrow when his wife, Mary, died in 1884. Two years later, he married Mina Miller, who would be his friend and partner for the rest of his life.

As Edison approached middle age, he pursued his dreams with his usual unflagging energy. In 1889, he began tinkering with a machine that would project moving pictures onto the wall. Before long, he had created the movie projector. This was by no means his last invention. Thomas Edison continued to experiment and invent for over forty more years. He became known to the nation as "the wizard of Menlo Park." During his lifetime, he patented 1,093 inventions, more than any other American inventor. His creations include the mimeograph, fluoroscope, alkaline storage battery, and dictating machine, as well as countless improvements to the telegraph, telephone, phonograph, and motion-picture projector. During World War I, Edison worked with the U.S. Navy on torpedo mechanisms and antisubmarine devices.

Thomas Edison died on October 18, 1931. He was eighty-four years old. His wife, Mina, turned out the light in their window to signal to the world that the great inventor was gone. In homes throughout the nation, people turned off their lights in silent homage to the man who had given us the electric light, and so much more.

JULIETTE GORDON LOW

∽

1860–1927

Founder of the Girl Scouts

Since March 12, 1912, an organization called the Girl Scouts of the U.S.A. has been creating opportunities for young women between the ages of five and seventeen to learn new skills, support their country, and reach out to girls in other countries. Over the years, the Girl Scouts have touched the lives of almost fifty-two million women. This was all made possible because one extraordinary woman, Juliette Gordon Low, refused to hear the word "no."

Juliette Gordon was born on October 31, 1860, in Savannah, Georgia. The second of six children, Juliette was an active, outgoing child with an eager sense of curiosity that led her into countless adventures. Early on, an uncle observed that the girl was "going to be a daisy," and for the rest of her life, Juliette Gordon was called "Daisy" by her family and friends.

Daisy's early years were overshadowed by the pain and suffering caused by the American Civil War. William Gordon, Daisy's father, was a captain in the Confederate army. While he fought for the South, Daisy's mother, Eleanor Kinzie Gordon, tried to keep the children safe in Savannah. As the war raged on, the Gordon children were often hungry, cold, and frightened. When Savannah was captured by soldiers from the North, Eleanor Gordon fled with the children to her parents' home in Chicago, Illinois. In Chicago, the family was safe and had plenty of food. The years of hunger, however, had made Daisy weak, and she grew very sick. Though Daisy recovered in time, she remained thin and small for her age.

At the war's end, the Gordon family returned to their home in Savannah. Though William Gordon's cotton business was almost entirely destroyed and their house was in a shambles, the family was happy to be together and safe. Slowly, William and Eleanor Gordon began rebuilding their lives.

For the Gordon children, the years following the Civil War were happy and full of adventures. Daisy enjoyed horseback riding, swimming, and tennis, as well as drawing and writing poetry. Putting her lively imagination to work, Daisy often led the other children in dramatic performances to entertain the adults.

At age thirteen, Daisy left home to attend Edge Hill Boarding School in Virginia. The young women at Daisy's school were expected to speak only in German and French, and the rules were very rigid. Daisy's playful antics were frowned upon by the teachers, though they quickly won her many friends among the students.

When Daisy graduated from Edge Hill at the age of seventeen, she entered Charbonnier's Finishing School in New York City. There, Daisy Gordon was taught all the skills that were expected of a wealthy Southern lady in the late 1870s. She learned lovely manners and she learned to dance, to curtsy, and to speak excellent French. After graduating from Charbonnier's School, Daisy returned to Savannah and entered the lavish, leisurely life of a true Savannah belle. Quick-witted, lively, and pretty, Daisy Gordon soon became one of the most popular young women in Savannah.

Daisy traveled to Europe for the first time in 1882. There she met William Low, a handsome young gentleman from a very wealthy family. The two quickly became good friends, and when Daisy returned to Europe two years later, that friendship turned to love.

Daisy was making plans for a sumptuous wedding when she suffered a great loss. Daisy's childhood illness had left her susceptible to infections. She awoke one morning with a terrible earache in one ear and, within days, Daisy's hearing in that ear was severely diminished.

Undaunted, Daisy continued to make plans. On December 21, 1866, Daisy (Juliette) Gordon and William Low were married. Their wedding was the social event of the season, but the celebration soon turned sorrowful. As Daisy and William ran through the hail of rice thrown by the wedding guests, a grain of rice settled in Daisy's good ear. The ensuing infection left Daisy nearly deaf in both ears.

After several months in Savannah, William began to yearn for his home in England, and the young couple decided to return to William's native land. As they crossed the ocean, Daisy was frightened. Without her hearing, how could she communicate with people in a new country?

Daisy need not have worried. Her clever stories and enthusiasm soon won her many friends in British society. Among Daisy's closest friends in her new home was the well-known author Rudyard Kipling. Daisy spent the next few years attending parties and traveling between her home in the United States and the homes she shared with William in England and Scotland. Though Daisy often had difficulty understanding what people were trying to say, she refused to let her deafness keep her from communicating with others.

Daisy's life was not as pleasant and carefree as it probably appeared to friends and acquaintances, however. William had begun to drink excessively, and their marriage was suffering. Daisy sought comfort in her artwork, learning to sculpt and to work with metal, but no amount of activity could improve her relationship with William. Just as Daisy and William Low were contemplating divorce, William died of ailments caused by his alcoholism.

For the first time, Daisy began to wish she had learned more useful skills than dancing and behaving like a "lady." She began to yearn for something meaningful to do with her life. She wanted to make a difference in the world.

In 1911, Daisy met a distinguished war hero named General Sir Robert Baden-Powell. Like Daisy, Sir Robert was a sculptor, and the two quickly became friends. Though Daisy could not have known it, Sir Robert was about to change her life.

Sir Robert Baden-Powell introduced Daisy to an organization he had founded for boys called the Boy Scouts. His sister, Agnes Baden-Powell, had formed a similar organization for English girls called the Girl Guides. The Girl Guides gave girls an opportunity to learn new skills and participate in useful activities.

Daisy was inspired. Before long, she had started a Girl Guides group near her home in Scotland. Daisy's Girl Guides were from very poor families and were expected to leave home at a very young age to begin earning money. Daisy taught the girls to raise poultry and spin yarn so that they could earn money for their families without leaving home. In just a few months, Daisy had made a difference.

Daisy wanted to introduce this program to girls in the United States. In 1912, she returned to Savannah and announced that she was forming the first Girl Guides group in the United States. Thanks to Daisy's enthusiasm, the idea caught on. Soon Daisy was forming additional groups and selecting women to lead them. If the women were reluctant or said no, Daisy simply pretended not to have heard. Daisy's Girl Guides began spreading across the country. In 1913, Daisy opened the national headquarters in Washington, D.C., and changed the name of the organization from Girl Guides to Girl Scouts.

When the United States entered World War I in 1917, Daisy sent a letter to the president offering the assistance of the Girl Scouts. Throughout the war, Daisy's girls collected food, helped the Red Cross, prepared bandages, and cared for small children so that mothers could work. Girls in every state wanted to join the Girl Scouts to help their country. By 1919, 150 girls were joining the Girl Scouts each day. Daisy's dream was becoming a reality.

At the war's end, Daisy traveled back to Europe to form an international office for Girl Scouts and Girl Guides. She believed that if young people of different countries grew to understand one another, they might never start another world war. Together with Baden-Powell and his wife Olave, Daisy formed the World Organization of Girl Guides and Girl Scouts.

Juliette Gordon Low, known to the world as Daisy, the founder of the Girl Scouts, died on January 17, 1927, after a long battle with cancer. Daisy lived long enough to see her Girl Scouts become a worldwide organization. At her request, Daisy was buried in her Girl Scout uniform.

HELEN KELLER

∽

1880–1968

Author, Activist

I
n 1904, a twenty-four-year-old woman named Helen Keller crossed the stage at Radcliffe College to receive her diploma. She was one graduating senior among many, but the audience burst into wild applause. To most of the spectators, Helen Keller's achievement seemed remarkable, almost miraculous. She had earned a college degree, despite the fact that she was both deaf and blind.

Helen Adams Keller was born on June 27, 1880, in Tuscumbia, Alabama. She was a curious, energetic child. Her parents, Arthur and Kate Keller, were delighted by Helen's quick mind.

When Helen was nineteen months old, she developed a high fever that lasted for several days. When she began to recover, the Kellers were devastated to find that she could no longer see or hear. She seemed to be alone in an unreachable world of silence and darkness. Because Helen could not hear, she did not learn to speak. As she grew older, she became increasingly frustrated by her inability to communicate. The Kellers had no idea how to teach her.

In 1887, when Helen was six years old, the Kellers hired Anne Sullivan to teach their daughter. Anne Sullivan had worked as a teacher at the Perkins

Institution, a school for blind children in Boston, Massachusetts. She once had been a student at Perkins herself. Until the age of fourteen, when an operation removed cataracts from her eyes, Anne Sullivan was almost totally blind. She had limited vision throughout her life.

At Perkins, Anne Sullivan had known Laura Bridgman, the first deaf-blind student ever educated in the United States. Anne learned everything she could about the methods used to teach Laura. But when she arrived in Alabama to meet Helen Keller, Anne Sullivan was on her own.

Anne Sullivan quickly realized that, despite their best intentions, Helen's parents were a major obstacle to her education. They felt so sorry for Helen that they spoiled her dreadfully. After a few days, Anne insisted that she and Helen move into a cabin not far from the family's house. Once she had Helen away from her parents, her teaching began in earnest.

At first, Helen resented her new teacher. She flung herself to the floor in violent tantrums. Yet she grew curious about the odd finger signals that the stranger constantly showed her. Anne Sullivan was trying to teach Helen the hand alphabet used by people who are deaf. In this "finger spelling," each letter is represented by a specific hand shape. Anne would hand Helen a doll and spell d-o-l-l into her hand. Helen learned this new game quickly. She imitated her teacher's hand shapes, but she did not understand that the signals spelled the name for the object she held.

Helen's breakthrough came on a bright April morning when Anne Sullivan had been with the Kellers for nearly a month. As Helen filled a mug at the water pump, Anne spelled w-a-t-e-r into her hand. Helen felt the water trickling through the fingers of one hand, and the letters being spelled into the other. Suddenly, she understood that the letters formed a word, and that the word represented the liquid that she was feeling. In that instant, Helen Keller discovered language, the key to the world around her.

Hungry to communicate with others, Helen wanted to know the names for everything she touched. Within a few weeks, she had learned to spell whole sentences with the hand alphabet. Anne Sullivan began teaching her to read and write in Braille. A code using raised dots, Braille is the reading method used by people who are blind.

Eventually, Anne Sullivan realized that Helen needed more education than Anne, alone, could provide. She persuaded the Kellers to let her take Helen to Perkins. Helen was happy at the school and plunged eagerly into her studies. Newspapers carried glowing accounts of her accomplishments, and letters poured in from admirers across the country. Some of the most famous men and women in America went to Perkins to meet her. The writer Mark Twain and the inventor Alexander Graham Bell, who developed the first telephone, became Helen's friends.

When she was ten, Helen announced that she wanted to learn to speak. This was a formidable challenge, since she could not hear the words she was trying to say. Anne Sullivan showed her how to move her lips and tongue in order to form each sound. Helen touched her teacher's throat to feel the vibrations from her voice and tried to make her own throat vibrate in the same way. Eventually, her speech was clear enough to be understood by people who knew her well, though strangers usually needed an interpreter.

At fourteen, Helen Keller entered the Write-Humanson School for the Deaf in New York, where she worked to improve her speech still further. Next she enrolled at the Cambridge School for Young Ladies, which she attended for four years. In the fall of 1900, Helen Keller entered Radcliffe College. Anne Sullivan was at her side, copying textbooks into Braille and spelling the teachers' words into Helen's hand. After four years of hard work, Helen Keller graduated with honors.

Helen Keller was aware that her road to success was made a little easier because she had become a celebrity. She also knew that few other disabled people were so fortunate. Most blind people lived in poverty and were treated by society as worthless outcasts. Those from rich families usually were sheltered from the world. Many parents felt that it was shameful to have a blind child, and

Helen Keller (left)
and Anne Sullivan

they tried to hide their blind sons or daughters in back rooms.

Upon graduating from college, Helen Keller dedicated herself to enhancing life for other people who were blind. She traveled throughout the country, lecturing and writing about the experience of being disabled. She used herself as an example of how much blind people could achieve when given the chance. She worked tirelessly to raise funds for the American Foundation for the Blind, an organization that sought to improve opportunities for blind people.

By reading and asking questions, and through her extensive travels, Helen Keller acquainted herself with all of the important social issues of her day. Throughout her life, she was a champion of the poor and the oppressed, whether they were blind or sighted. She wrote articles in support of labor unions and called for better conditions for people in city slums. Critics claimed that she had no right to speak out on such topics. She couldn't see, so what could she know about slum conditions? Helen Keller was frustrated to learn that the public wanted her to focus on her own life, to stay away from controversy.

In 1904, the year she graduated from Radcliffe, Helen Keller's first book was published, an autobiography entitled *The Story of My Life.* Years later she continued her story in *Midstream.* Her book *Teacher* is a tribute to her teacher and friend Anne Sullivan, who died in 1936.

During World War II, Helen Keller visited wounded soldiers in hospitals and rehabilitation centers. She encouraged the soldiers who had lost their sight to believe that they could live full, satisfying lives. In 1963, she was awarded the Presidential Medal of Freedom.

Helen Keller gave a voice to millions of disabled people around the world, people who had been pushed aside and forgotten throughout most of human history. Through her own life, she proved that people with disabilities could be active and independent, that they could take their place as valued members of the community. When she died in 1968, she was universally hailed as one of the great leaders of the twentieth century.

FRANKLIN DELANO ROOSEVELT

∽

1882–1945

U.S. President

In 1932, the United States was in the midst of the Great Depression. More than fifteen million people were unemployed. Families were hungry, and many banks were failing. The country, desperately in need of a strong leader, turned to Franklin Delano Roosevelt. On March 4, 1933, Franklin Delano Roosevelt became the thirty-second president of the United States of America. Roosevelt promised a "New Deal" for the American people. He introduced bold new measures designed to create jobs for the unemployed and give assistance to those in need. Under Roosevelt's leadership, the country gradually emerged from the Great Depression.

Franklin Delano Roosevelt was, in many ways, an unlikely champion of the poor and needy. The son of a successful New York lawyer, he grew up surrounded by wealth and comfort. His mother, Sara Delano Roosevelt, was extremely protective of her only son. Franklin received his early education at home from private tutors. He was fourteen before he left home to attend Groton, a private school in Massachusetts.

At Groton, Franklin was profoundly influenced by the headmaster, Endicott Peabody. Peabody taught his pupils that the wealthy have a responsibility to help the less fortunate. This philosophy was to become the cornerstone of Roosevelt's New Deal.

At age eighteen, Roosevelt entered Harvard University. He was, at best, an average student. He was most interested in editing the undergraduate newspaper, the *Crimson*.

While at Harvard, Franklin met a distant cousin, Eleanor Roosevelt. A social worker in New York's East Side slums, Eleanor showed Franklin the miserable living conditions of the poor in New York City. He was deeply disturbed by the suffering he observed. Franklin's respect for this compassionate young woman soon turned to affection. They were married on March 17, 1905.

After graduating from Harvard, Roosevelt attended Columbia Law School. He passed the bar examination in 1907 and went to work for a law firm in New York. In 1911, Roosevelt left his law practice when he was elected as a New York state senator. He held this office for seven years before President Woodrow Wilson appointed him assistant secretary of the navy.

In August 1921, illness interrupted Roosevelt's career. After a day of sailing, he went to bed suffering from chills. Within a few days, he was completely paralyzed. At age thirty-nine, Franklin Delano Roosevelt had contracted polio. Eventually he grew strong enough to use crutches for walking short distances, but Roosevelt never regained the full use of his legs.

Many thought Roosevelt's political career had come to a close, but Roosevelt had no intention of giving up. The man who once had announced, "There's nothing I like better than a good fight," was fighting. After three painful years of physical therapy, Franklin Delano Roosevelt resumed his law practice and his political activities.

In 1929, Roosevelt became the governor of the state of New York. Roosevelt's relief programs helped the people of New York during the early years of the Great Depression and earned him the respect of the nation. In 1932, Roosevelt announced his candidacy for president.

Though the American public knew that Roosevelt had had polio, he worked very hard to hide the extent of his disability. He believed that people would not give their full confidence to a man who could not walk. During public appearances, Roosevelt took his son's arm. Though it looked as if they were simply standing or walking side by side, his son was actually supporting his father's weight. The press cooperated in hiding Roosevelt's disability. Of the thousands of official photographs taken of Roosevelt during his presidency, only two showed him using a wheelchair.

At the time, Roosevelt chose the course he believed would best serve his political career and the nation as a whole. Yet today many people feel that a great opportunity was lost when Roosevelt decided to hide his disability. Instead of presenting himself as a highly competent and authoritative person who was disabled, Roosevelt tried to look like a man who was hardly disabled at all.

During his first two terms as president, Franklin Delano Roosevelt con-

President Roosevelt rarely allowed photographers to take pictures that would reveal his disability.

Franklin Delano Roosevelt

centrated on eliminating the country's financial woes. He almost had succeeded in restoring the nation's confidence when, near the end of his second term, war erupted in Europe. Again, the American people turned to Franklin Delano Roosevelt for direction.

In November 1940, Roosevelt was reelected, becoming the only president in American history to serve three terms. On December 7, 1941, the Japanese attacked Pearl Harbor, and America entered World War II. Throughout the war, Franklin Delano Roosevelt was a source of strength and inspiration for the people of America. In 1944, he was elected to an unprecedented fourth term.

On April 12, 1945, as World War II was coming to an end, Franklin Delano Roosevelt passed away. He had served his country through its darkest days, and his death was a source of sorrow to people throughout the world.

HORACE PIPPIN

∽

1888–1946

Artist

The son of an African-American laborer, Horace Pippin was born in West Chester, Pennsylvania. In his youth, his family moved to Goshen, New York. As a boy, Horace liked to visit the local racetrack. While he enjoyed the excitement of the races, he loved most of all to sketch the galloping horses. He wanted to capture their grace and beauty on paper and worked patiently to get the details right.

After completing the eighth grade, Horace dropped out of school to help his family. Over the next fifteen years, he took an assortment of jobs—farmhand, junk dealer, furniture mover. He still loved to draw, but he worked long, hard hours and had almost no time for such luxuries.

In 1917, the United States entered World War I, the terrible conflict that was raging in Europe. Horace Pippin joined the New York National Guard. Within months, he embarked for France with the all-black 369th Infantry. Horace found himself on the front lines of the fighting. Amid the thunder of shelling and the moans of dying men, he kept a diary on five-cent notepads. For the rest of his life, this record of his war experiences provided Pippin with images to transform into paintings.

In September 1918, two months before the end of the fighting, a shell fragment shattered Pippin's right shoulder. Army doctors replaced the splintered bone with a steel plate, but the injury left Pippin's right arm almost totally paralyzed. In May 1919, he was released from the hospital and shipped back to the United States. The medical report declared him unfit for work because of his disability.

Pippin settled in West Chester, Pennsylvania, the town of his birth. In 1920, he married Ora Giles, a widow with a young son. The couple moved into a redbrick row house, living on Pippin's disability pension and the money his wife earned by taking in laundry. Pippin soon became a pillar of the community. He sang in the church choir, organized a Boy Scout troop, and was elected commander of West Chester's black American Legion post.

The horrors of the war haunted Horace Pippin, and sometimes he sank into deep depression. As therapy for his right arm, and to gain some control over the memories that tortured him, he tried to draw again. At first, he experimented with charcoal drawings on the lids of wooden cigar boxes. Later he developed a unique method of engraving on wooden panels with a red-hot iron poker. Gripping the poker in his immobile right hand, he braced the panel against his knee and moved it with his left hand, burning an image into the wood. Sometimes he enlivened these designs with touches of paint. Years later he explained that art "brought me back to my old self."

After working with wood engravings for twelve years, Pippin found that his right arm had grown stronger. Now he experimented with painting. Supporting his right wrist with his left hand, he held the brush in his right hand and moved it across the canvas. He worked very slowly, with painstaking care, building up layer upon layer of paint to create the effects he wanted. He used the most inexpensive materials he could find, working with house paints on a homemade easel.

In 1931, Pippin began his first major work, *The End of the War: Starting Home*. He spent three years on the painting, which depicts German soldiers surrendering amid a hail of bursting shells. To convey the impression of bomb-torn earth, he sometimes laid down as many as one hundred layers of paint. Other early paintings, such as *Shell Holes and Observation Balloons: Champagne Sector and Dogfight over the Trenches*, also express the torment of war. "[The war] brought out all the art in me," Pippin explained later. "I came home with all of it in my mind, and I paint from it today."

At first, only Pippin's friends knew about his work, but in 1935, he came to the attention of Dr. Christian Brinton of the West Chester Art Center. Brinton supplied Pippin with proper oil paints, and in 1937 arranged an exhibition of his work at the West Chester Community Center. The following year, the New York Museum of Modern Art included four of Pippin's pictures in an exhibition entitled *Masters of Popular Painting*. The public was so enthusiastic that Pippin soon had one-man shows in Philadelphia, New York, Chicago, and San Francisco.

By the 1940s, Pippin had begun to explore new subjects in his work. He painted landscapes, flowers, and scenes of African-American family life. "Pictures just come to mind," he told a reporter. "I think my pictures out with my brain, then tell my heart to go ahead. If the idea is worthwhile, I paint it. I go over the picture in my mind several times, and then I start painting."

As the world plunged into yet another devastating war—World War II—Pippin's paintings expressed a passionate longing for peace. In *The Holy Mountain*, a painting with a biblical theme, he included a row of white crosses such as those that mark the graves of fallen soldiers. "As more men are dying today, the little crosses tell us of them in the First World War, and all that we are going through now," he explained. "But there will be peace."

Pippin's work continued to earn praise in the most prestigious circles of the art world. But Pippin seemed almost untouched by the excitement that spiraled around him. He did not paint to achieve fame and wealth. As he stated, "My opinion of art is that a man paints from his heart and mind."

When Horace Pippin died in 1946, he had completed more than 150 paintings, drawings, and wood-panel engravings. His works were displayed in private collections and in some of the finest museums in the United States. But in the decades that followed, the public forgot the quiet man who evoked the anguish of war with layers of house paint. Then, in 1994, the Metropolitan Museum of Art in New York displayed one hundred of the artist's works in a show that aroused a fresh burst of interest in Horace Pippin and his work. A new generation of Americans recognized the unique talent of the man who held out the promise that "there will be peace."

Dorothea Lange

∽

1895-1965

Photographer

"Walk as well as you can," Dorothea Lange's mother would say whenever they went out together. Her mother's words stung. Dorothea had had polio when she was seven years old, and forever after the illness, she walked with a limp. She felt that her mother was ashamed of her appearance, and she grew painfully self-conscious. It made matters worse when other children teased her and called her "Limpy." Though her disability was relatively minor, Dorothea was always aware of it. Near the end of her life she explained, "I think it was perhaps the most important thing that happened to me. It formed me, guided me, instructed me, helped me, and humiliated me, all those things at once. I've never gotten over it, and I am aware of the force and power of it."

Dorothea grew up in Hoboken, New Jersey. Her parents were divorced when she was twelve, and her mother took a job in New York City. Dorothea commuted with her mother, attending junior and senior high school in Manhattan. She was not an enthusiastic student, but she found the city fascinating. Sometimes she slipped out of class to spend hours exploring the streets. As she peered into shop windows and studied the faces of passersby, she felt as though she were invisible. She was a silent observer of the life around her. She hungered to make a record of everything she saw, to capture fleeting moments on film. Years later she commented, "I had never not been sure that I was a photographer, any more than you would not be sure that you were yourself!"

Dorothea's mother thought her dream of becoming a photographer was hopelessly impractical. She wanted Dorothea to learn a trade that would promise a steady salary. Reluctantly, Dorothea enrolled in a teachers' college. But on evenings and weekends, she took a series of jobs in photographers' studios. She was an eager apprentice and learned everything she could about taking and developing pictures.

When Dorothea was eighteen, she announced that she was going to travel around the world, finding work along the way. With her camera slung from her shoulder, she set out on her great adventure. She got only as far as San Francisco, where her wallet was stolen and she was left almost penniless. Based on her experience in New York, she quickly found a job as a photographer's assistant. Soon she belonged to a thriving community of photographers and artists. For the rest of her life, Dorothea Lange made her home in northern California.

Within a few years, Dorothea opened her own photography studio. Some of the most prominent families in the San Francisco area commissioned her to take their portraits. In 1920, she married Maynard Dixon, a well-known artist who painted Western scenes. They had two sons, Daniel and John.

During the 1930s, the United States was mired in a disastrous economic depression. Banks and factories closed, and millions of people lost their jobs. Desperate men and women lined up for free soup and bread from the Salvation Army and other charities. Few people could afford family portraits any longer, and Dorothea's business sagged. She filled her days by walking the streets and taking pictures of the hungry and homeless.

In 1935, people from Oklahoma and Arkansas began streaming into California. A devastating drought had destroyed their livelihood. Their land had become a

This is perhaps the most famous photograph taken by Dorothea Lange. It shows the distress of a woman during the Great Depression.

Dust Bowl, and they headed west in search of work. Many moved from place to place, picking grapes, peaches, or peas—whatever crop was in season. When they had work, they crowded into run-down shacks without electricity or running water. When they had no work, they starved. Then the U.S. Department of Agriculture launched a program to resettle many of these migrant workers on cooperative farms. Dorothea Lange was hired to document the conditions of California farmworkers in photographs.

Lange's photographs appeared in countless government reports and in newspapers and magazines across the country. They told the heartbreaking story of people who had lost everything but their dignity. Some of her pictures, such as *Migrant Mother* and *White Angel Bread Line*, were printed again and again. They became symbols of humanity's power to rise above grief and suffering. As Dorothea's son, Daniel Dixon, wrote, "Ugliness and horror are not really the subjects of her photographs, but the people to whom ugliness and horror have happened. Her attention is not given to misery but to the miserable. Her concern is not with affliction but with the afflicted."

Dorothea Lange's work soon took her beyond California, to photograph Mississippi sharecroppers and Oklahoma ghost towns. Wherever she went, she put people at ease, winning their confidence before she began to snap pictures. "Being disabled gave me an immense advantage," she said, looking back. "It puts you on a different level than if you go into a situation whole and secure." She always felt that her disability was a major influence in the work she chose to do. "We all have those things that form us," she said. "They are our architecture, and there is much we don't know. I mean, this is only a part of it. But the explanation of a person's work sometimes hinges on just such a succession of incidents. And those incidents dictate our responses. My acceptance finally of my lameness truly opened gates for me."

On December 7, 1941, Japanese planes bombed the U.S. naval fleet at Pearl Harbor in Hawaii. The United States plunged into World War II. The U.S. government feared that Japanese-Americans on the West Coast would be disloyal and forced them into detention camps. Dorothea Lange visited the camps and created a rich photographic document of life behind the barbed-wire fences. Once again, her pictures showed pain, sadness, and the immense will to survive.

In the early 1940s, Dorothea Lange developed severe stomach ulcers. For the last twenty years of her life, she was in and out of hospitals, where she underwent numerous operations and radiation treatments. Her illness made traveling difficult, but she continued to work close to home. In 1963, the Museum of Modern Art in New York announced plans for a retrospective exhibition of Dorothea Lange's work. Though she was gravely ill with cancer by this time, Lange sorted through thousands of negatives, selected pictures, and wrote captions. She did not live to see the exhibition open, but she left behind a priceless legacy—three decades of American history preserved in pictures for future generations to study and admire.

FRIDA KAHLO

1907–1954

Artist

F rida Kahlo is known throughout the world for her unique and sometimes disturbing paintings. Her art was recognized in her lifetime and
continues to intrigue art lovers today. Both during and after her life,
however, people have been as fascinated with Frida as with her paintings.

Frida Kahlo was a small, slim woman with thick, dark hair and heavy eye-
brows that nearly met in the middle of her forehead. She dressed in long,
brightly colored skirts, the traditional apparel of women from Tehuantepec, a
city in southern Mexico. She wore exotic jewelry and wove ribbons into her
long, black braids. Frida Kahlo's personality was as dramatic as her clothing.
She had keen intelligence and was completely unafraid to speak her mind. She
also had an impish sense of humor and a warm heart, which endeared her to
people of all ages. Throughout her many years of physical suffering, Frida
remained committed to living life as boldly and vividly as she painted.

Magdalena Carmen Frida Kahlo y Calderon, called "Frida," was born in
Coyoacan, Mexico, on July 6, 1907. As a child, Frida was bright and mischievous,
often surprising her family with funny pranks. Though Frida was a playful child,
her early years were often difficult. Her father, who had a head injury in his youth,

suffered frequent seizures. Because her mother also was in poor health, Frida and her younger sister usually were cared for by their older sisters. When Frida was six years old, she contracted polio. She became very ill and did not recover for nearly nine months. When at last she was well, Frida's right leg was withered and very weak. Nevertheless, Frida remained an active and fearless child.

Frida's father, Guillermo Kahlo, was proud of his intelligent daughter. He was determined to provide her with an excellent education. At fourteen, Frida entered the National Preparatory School, which was considered one of the finest schools in Mexico. She was one of just thirty-five girls enrolled at the school along with nearly two thousand boys. At school, Frida made many friends. She also began to study for a career in medicine. These were happy years for young Frida Kahlo, but her happiness was not to last.

On September 17, 1925, when Frida was eighteen years old, she and her good friend Alejandro Gomez Arias were in a horrible bus accident. Alejandro was only slightly injured, but Frida was not so fortunate. Her body was completely pierced by the bus handrail. Her spinal column was broken in three places, her collarbone was broken, her right leg was fractured, and her foot was crushed. For days, her doctors and family did not think she would live. Frida survived, but she suffered from her injuries for the rest of her life.

After the bus accident, Frida spent a month in the hospital and was confined to her bed for three additional months. To fill the long hours of boredom and loneliness, Frida began to paint. Her first painting was a self-portrait that revealed her inner feelings about her body. "From the time [of the accident], my obsession was to begin again, painting things just as I saw them with my own eyes and nothing more," said Frida.

Frida's recovery was very slow. She could not resume a normal life until 1927. Even then, Frida did not return to her medical studies. Her pain was too intense, and she had developed a greater love than medicine—painting. At this time, Frida also grew interested in the political issues of her country. She joined her friends from the National Preparatory School in a battle against the rule of

Mexico's military dictator. This cause eventually led her to join the Communist Party, where she met Diego Rivera, a famous Mexican painter. Like Frida, Diego wanted to wrench control of Mexico from the hands of the military and return it to the Mexican people. Although Rivera was twenty years older than Frida, they fell in love and were married on August 21, 1929.

Frida's relationship with Diego Rivera became a central theme in her paintings. Theirs was a difficult marriage. They separated several times. In 1939, they divorced, but they remarried the following year. Despite their many difficulties, Frida Kahlo and Diego Rivera remained deeply attached to one another throughout Frida's lifetime.

Another theme in Frida's paintings was her own physical suffering. Frida painted graphic, disturbing pictures of her own wounds. In both her life and in her painting, Frida Kahlo was determined to face the truth squarely, with courage and honesty.

In the early years of her marriage, Frida's paintings were overshadowed by her husband's renowned murals. As Frida gained more confidence, however, her own work began to gain attention from the art world. In 1938, she went to New York City for the first major showing of her art. After her New York debut, Kahlo's paintings were admired by artists and intellectuals throughout the United States and Europe.

In her adult years, Frida Kahlo underwent thirty-two surgical operations on her spine and her foot. She spent much of her life in hospitals or in bed at home, bound in stiff corsets, as her back healed from major operations. For long periods, the only way Frida could paint was while sitting up in bed. Despite these obstacles, she gained international acclaim for her painting. She also remained active in politics and, in later years, taught young artists.

Frida Kahlo died on July 13, 1954, at the age of forty-seven, but her paintings continue to be studied and admired. With courage and a great love of life, she was able to transform her suffering into images that continue to speak to art lovers today.

SIR DOUGLAS BADER

1910–1982

Pilot, War Hero

Douglas Bader loved to fly, loved his country, and loved a challenge. A British hero in World War II, Bader was awarded both the Distinguished Service Order and the Distinguished Flying Cross for leadership and valor in action. As a fighter pilot and wing commander in Great Britain's Royal Air Force, Douglas Bader introduced fighting tactics that saved the lives of many British pilots. He also was credited with shooting down at least twenty-four enemy planes. Though he lost both legs in a plane crash several years before World War II, Douglas Bader refused to be defeated by his disability.

Douglas Robert Stuart Bader, the second son of Frederick and Jessie Bader, was born on February 21, 1910, in London, England. Soon after Bader's birth, his parents left for India, taking their older son, Derick, with them. Douglas remained in England with relatives because he was too young to travel. He was nearly two years old before he joined his family in India. The Bader family returned to England in 1913. When World War I began the following year, Bader's father left to join the fighting. Douglas Bader's father did not return from the war.

While the war was being fought, Douglas Bader attended preparatory school. Though bright, Douglas was not a devoted student. Instead, he excelled in athletic activities. He was such a good athlete that he was named captain of his school's cricket and rugby teams. After his father's death, however, Bader realized he would need an academic scholarship to attend a good school. Douglas Bader rose to the challenge. He applied himself to his studies and earned a scholarship to St. Edward's School, near Oxford.

Douglas was happy at St. Edward's. As before, he neglected his studies, but he was very good at sports. At fifteen, he became the youngest player on both the cricket and rugby teams. Douglas Bader was seventeen when he decided he wanted to become a pilot in the Royal Air Force (RAF). Unfortunately, the tuition at Cranwell, the RAF college, was too expensive for his family.

Cranwell offered six scholarships each year, and Douglas Bader was determined to earn one of them. Once again, Douglas turned to his books. After months of hard work, he won a place at Cranwell, where he became one of the most promising pilots of his class (as well as one of the finest rugby players). In 1930, Pilot Officer Bader graduated near the top of his class and officially joined the RAF.

Douglas Bader loved squadron life. He was renowned for his skill in aerobatics, or trick flying. Bader was very talented, but he was also overconfident. On December 14, 1931, when he was only twenty-one years old, Bader accepted a dare that would change his life. He attempted to do a very low turn in a plane that was not built for trick flying. The plane crashed, and Bader was nearly killed. His legs were crushed and had to be amputated. For days, doctors wondered whether the young man would survive.

Bader recovered slowly. As he regained strength, he began moving about with the help of crutches and a temporary "peg leg." Douglas was determined to go on with his life. Against hospital rules, he began learning how to drive a car with the artificial leg. Douglas Bader took long drives with friends from the hospital. On one such outing, Bader and his companions stopped for tea at a

Sir Douglas Bader boarding an RAF fighter plane in 1950

restaurant called The Pantiles. The waitress, a dignified young woman named Thelma Edwards, caught Bader's attention. After that day, Douglas visited The Pantiles regularly, and his friendship with Thelma gradually grew into a romance.

When at last Bader was well enough to be fitted with permanent artificial legs, called prostheses, he was told that he would need a cane to help him walk. Douglas Bader stubbornly insisted that he would never walk with a stick. After many weeks of frustrating practice, Bader learned to walk without a cane. He was ready for a new challenge.

Bader resolved to show the RAF that he could fly without legs. He was sent to Central Flying School, where he proved that he was an excellent pilot, with or without legs. But RAF regulations did not permit legless pilots, so Bader was forced to retire from the air force. Douglas Bader was discouraged, but he did not despair. He soon found a position in the aviation section of a petroleum company. During this time, Bader did something he had wanted to do since his first visit to The Pantiles. He took Thelma Edwards dancing. Their relationship blossomed, and on October 5, 1933, Douglas Bader and Thelma Edwards were married.

Douglas Bader never gave up his dream of flying again. When World War II began in 1939, Bader was accepted into the Royal Air Force again. He had a natural ability to lead and was quickly promoted. Douglas Bader soon became a legend. Newspapers carried stories about the "legless hero." The pilots under his command were encouraged by his fearlessness and his sense of humor. His squadron was so successful at destroying enemy planes that it was nicknamed the "disintegration squadron."

Bader continued to fly for nearly two years without a rest. His wife and his superiors urged him to take a brief vacation, but Bader refused. In August 1941, his plane was hit by enemy fire over France. As his plane plunged toward the ground, Bader jumped, using a parachute to land safely. After being captured by German soldiers, Bader was taken to St. Omer Hospital. Confident that a disabled man could not escape, the Germans did not watch Bader closely. They had underestimated their prisoner. Bader tied bed sheets together to form a rope and escaped through the window. After two days of frantic searching, the Germans found Bader at a nearby farm and transported him to Germany. Bader continued his efforts to escape and nearly succeeded three different times. He finally was sent to Colditz, a German camp for troublesome, but important, prisoners. He remained there until the end of the war. In April 1945, Allied soldiers reached Colditz and freed the prisoners. After more than three years of captivity, Bader was reunited with his wife.

After the war, Bader returned to his old job at Shell Petroleum Company. In the years that followed, he tried to use his own experience to help others with disabilities. He visited hospitals and offered encouragement to people who had lost limbs. In 1976, Douglas Bader was knighted for his efforts on behalf of people with disabilities. After retiring from Shell in 1969, Bader continued to work to improve the lives of disabled individuals.

Even after Douglas Bader's death in 1982, he is remembered as a war hero. But his heroism did not end with the war. His courage and determination continued to inspire others throughout his life. Douglas Bader's example helped many other disabled individuals realize that they, too, could achieve their goals.

JACOBUS TENBROEK

1911–1968

Educator, Activist

A s a young man, Jacobus tenBroek's father immigrated to North America from the Netherlands. When Jacobus was born, his father was homesteading on the prairies of Alberta, Canada. Jacobus's first home was a log cabin with a dirt floor. Within a few years, the family had built the first frame house in the region.

Harvest season on the prairie was a time for neighbors to gather in celebration. At the harvest festivities when Jacobus was seven years old, someone drew a target on the side of a tent, and the children practiced shooting with bows and arrows. Jacobus went into the tent and tried to peer out at his friends through a hole in the target. At that moment, a boy let loose an arrow. The arrow sped to the target and pierced Jacobus's eye.

In 1918, there were few doctors in rural Canada. Without proper treatment, Jacobus quickly lost the vision of the injured eye. Within a few months, the other eye also was affected, and Jacobus tenBroek became totally blind.

The tenBroeks knew that their son would need a good education if he was ever to make his way in the world. Soon after the accident the family moved to California and enrolled Jacobus at the state-run California School for the Blind in Berkeley. One of the teachers was Dr. Newel Perry, a brilliant mathematician. Perry, who was blind himself, inspired his students to set high personal goals. He believed that blind people could compete with the sighted on equal terms, and he encouraged his students to become as independent as possible.

Jacobus tenBroek attended public high school in Berkeley. He was active in the student government and was a member of the debating team. After graduation, he went on to the University of California at Berkeley, where he majored in history. With Dr. Perry's encouragement, he attended law school at Berkeley.

Many law students helped to pay their expenses by teaching undergraduate classes in political science. Since he did not have much money, Jacobus tenBroek applied for one of these teaching positions. Although he had excellent grades and references, his application was turned down. "Blind people can't teach," he was told. "The university will never hire you." TenBroek knew that he could be a good teacher, if only he had the chance to prove himself. He volunteered to teach for a semester without pay, and the university accepted his offer. The school was so impressed by his teaching ability that the next semester he was hired.

TenBroek was fascinated by the history of law in the United States and wanted to teach at a university. After receiving his law degree, he applied for teaching jobs at some five hundred colleges and universities across the country. Based on his credentials, many of these schools were eager to have him. First, however, he had to appear for a personal interview. As soon as the hiring committee discovered that he was blind, the doors slammed shut. Despite his success at Berkeley, no one believed that he could teach.

Unable to find a teaching position, Jacobus tenBroek decided to pursue further studies. He won a Brandeis Research Fellowship to Harvard University, where he earned a postgraduate law degree. He also received a doctorate in law from Berkeley. Finally he obtained his first full-time teaching job in the law school at the University of Chicago.

Though he continued to build a rewarding career at the University of Chicago, Jacobus tenBroek remained frustrated. He knew that few other blind people were as fortunate as he was. Not many employers would consider hiring blind workers. Most blind people struggled to survive on tiny government stipends. The grants were so low that blind people lived in poverty.

In 1940, tenBroek helped to plan a meeting of blind men and women from seven states. The sixteen delegates gathered in Wilkes-Barre, Pennsylvania, to discuss the problems of blind Americans and to consider solutions. They concluded that blind people needed an organization that could voice their concerns to state and federal officials. The Wilkes-Barre convention was the founding session of the National Federation of the Blind (NFB). Jacobus tenBroek was elected to serve as the federation's first president. In his acceptance speech, tenBroek declared, "It is necessary for the blind to organize themselves and their ideas on a national basis, so that blind [people] the nation over can live in physical comfort, social dignity, and spiritual self-respect."

TenBroek, his wife Hazel, and their children returned to Berkeley, California, in 1942. For the next nineteen years, tenBroek was chairman of the Department of Speech at the university. The speech department offered study in a wide variety of subjects, including history, political science, and law. All these topics of study,

Jacobus tenBroek is remembered as an inspiring public speaker.

Jacobus tenBroek

tenBroek believed, were closely linked. In the speech department, what mattered most was freedom of expression. Under his direction, the department became one of the most exciting intellectual centers on campus.

Busy as he was with his work and family, tenBroek remained committed to the National Federation of the Blind. He never forgot the discrimination he had encountered when he was looking for a job. He was painfully aware that blind people all over the country faced similar indignities every day. Blind people were not permitted to serve on juries because they were deemed incompetent. They could not buy life insurance because they were thought to be accident-prone. In some states, they were forbidden by law from teaching in the public schools. TenBroek led the federation to battle these, and many other, injustices. He encouraged blind people everywhere to believe in themselves, and he worked to break down society's stereotypes about what the blind could do. He saw discrimination against blind people as a violation of their rights as guaranteed in the U.S. Constitution.

As the years passed, tenBroek was recognized as a national authority in the field of constitutional law. His first book, *Antislavery Origins of the Fourteenth Amendment,* appeared in 1951. In 1955, he published *Prejudice, War, and the Constitution,* about the internment of Japanese-Americans during World War II. The book won the prestigious Woodrow Wilson Foundation Award. Many of tenBroek's books and articles still are used by students of law today. In 1961, tenBroek resigned as president of the National Federation of the Blind. He was reelected in 1966 and served until his death from cancer two years later.

In 1992, a group of tenBroek's former students gathered in San Francisco to honor him at a memorial dinner. More than 170 attended. With loving words, they recalled tenBroek's generosity, his sense of humor, and his dedication to teaching and learning. In his memory, they established the TenBroek Society, which funds two scholarships each year. The society works to keep alive tenBroek's ideas about free speech and his view of constitutional principles as the foundation of American democracy.

Jacobus tenBroek

HAROLD RUSSELL

∞

1914–

Actor, Disability Rights Advocate

arold Russell was thirteen years old in 1927, when Charles A. Lindbergh made his heroic solo flight across the Atlantic Ocean. Like millions of other Americans, Harold was dazzled by Lindbergh's achievement. He dreamed of becoming a pilot like "Lindy," his hero, and doing daring deeds in the air.

Harold Russell was born in Nova Scotia, Canada. His father died when he was six years old, and his mother moved the family to Cambridge, Massachusetts. From the age of ten, Harold worked at odd jobs after school to help with the family finances. When he was a senior in high school, he applied to the Massachusetts Institute of Technology (MIT), hoping to study engineering. To his disappointment, he was not accepted. Instead of becoming an engineer, he took a job at a grocery store. Over the years that followed, Russell was promoted several times until he was the store manager.

In December 1941, the United States entered World War II. Harold Russell, who had longed for adventure as a boy, enlisted in the army and volunteered for paratrooper service. He was not sent overseas, but spent the war years as an instructor in stateside parachute and demolition schools. As a parachute instructor at Fort Benning, Georgia, Russell made fifty-one jumps.

The world remembers June 6, 1944, as D day, the day the Allied troops launched a massive assault on German-occupied France. Thousands of men died or were wounded in the vast D-day battle. On that same day, at Fort McCall, North Carolina, Sergeant Harold Russell was training a demolition squad in the use of TNT. Suddenly an explosion ripped the air. The charge that Russell was holding blew up in his hands because of a defective fuse. The following day, both of Russell's shattered hands were amputated.

Russell spent the following year at Walter Reed Army Hospital in Washington, D.C. Doctors fitted him with a pair of artificial hands, but he found them clumsy and useless. Instead he used a pair of hook-like prostheses that enabled him to grasp and manipulate objects easily. At first, Russell rejected the prosthetic hooks because they looked strange and unnatural. But eventually he realized they would give him the widest range of options. Slowly and painfully, Harold Russell adjusted to life without hands. Sometimes he felt deeply discouraged, convinced that he never could live fully again. He dreaded the pitying, horrified stares he knew he would face when he returned to the outside world. But as he learned to feed and dress himself, he began to understand that he need not be limited by his disability. He realized that he could pursue whatever goal he chose.

Shortly before he left Walter Reed, a movie crew visited the hospital. Russell was selected to play the leading role in a short documentary film, *Diary of a Sergeant*, the story of a soldier's rehabilitation after losing his hands. Much of the script was based on Russell's own experiences. The final scenes showed him leaving the hospital and enrolling at Boston University.

Diary of a Sergeant caught the attention of Hollywood movie producer Samuel Goldwyn, who was developing a feature film entitled *The Best Years of Our Lives*. The movie would tell the stories of several veterans returning home from World War II. One of those veterans is Homer Parrish, a sailor who loses his hands in battle. Goldwyn was so impressed with Russell's performance in

Diary of a Sergeant that he offered him the role of Parrish in the new movie. Russell took a leave of absence from college and moved to Hollywood.

In *The Best Years of Our Lives*, Homer Parrish was presented as a symbol of courage. The public was comfortable with this view of the disabled as people who strive heroically to overcome the obstacles that fate has set in their path. But the movie also touched upon aspects of disability that Hollywood rarely portrayed. It showed that people with disabilities faced the cruel stares of strangers and were rejected for jobs even when they were highly qualified. It suggested that prejudice was an even greater barrier than physical limitation.

The film was released in November 1946, and it became an instant box-office success. Though Russell had no formal training as an actor, critics raved about his performance. *The Best Years of Our Lives* won eight Academy Awards. Russell received two Oscars—a traditional award for Best Supporting Actor, and an honorary award for "bringing aid and comfort to disabled veterans through the medium of motion pictures."

Harold Russell, the former grocery-store manager, was famous overnight. He toured the country, addressing veterans' groups and civic organizations. His stardom gave him the opportunity to urge employers to hire people with disabilities. He also called for an end to racial discrimination. He argued that the country needed the talents and abilities of all its citizens. "Discrimination," he insisted, "is like amputating America's hands." In 1948, Russell took a position with the Anti-Defamation League of B'nai B'rith, an organization that works to combat anti-Semitism. The job enabled him to continue promoting racial understanding.

Russell's concern for disabled veterans led to his involvement with the World Veterans Federation (WVF), an international organization of veterans' associations. The WVF represented 160 associations from more than 50 countries. In 1951, Russell became vice chairman in charge of rehabilitation. That same year, he was elected vice president of the World Veterans Fund, which raised money to support the WVF. Russell traveled throughout the world, help-

Harold Russell in the 1960s, when he was chairman of the President's Committee on Employment for the Handicapped

ing to develop rehabilitation programs. He became an expert on prostheses, exercise equipment, and the philosophy of the rehabilitation movement. "The purpose of rehabilitation," he explained, "is to get handicapped persons back on the job as quickly as possible."

In April 1964, President Lyndon B. Johnson appointed Harold Russell chairman of the President's Committee on Employment of the Handicapped. Under Russell's leadership, the committee worked to educate employers about the capabilities of disabled people. Russell tried to persuade employers that it was in their own interest to hire people with disabilities. He cited statistics to prove that disabled workers generally were more loyal and productive than those who were not disabled. Russell recognized that the best prostheses in the world were useless if people with disabilities were denied opportunities. He worked ceaselessly to enhance the lives of people with disabilities and, in so doing, to build a better society for everyone.

THE FIGHT FOR DISABILITY RIGHTS LEGISLATION

⌒⌒

When Greg Solas went to the polls in Warwick, Rhode Island, in 1988, he confronted a long flight of stairs. For Solas and other wheelchair users, the polling place was totally inaccessible. Election officials told Solas that he could fill out his ballot while he sat in his car. But he pointed out that, by law, the election must be held in a place that was accessible to all citizens. He had the right to go to the polls and vote like everyone else.

Greg Solas filed a suit against the local board of elections under the Rhode Island Human Rights Act. This state law prohibits discrimination against minority groups, including people with disabilities. After a barrage of hearings and paperwork, Solas won his case. From that time on, elections in Warwick were held in buildings with ramps and elevators. Soon, other Rhode Island communities made similar changes.

A former ironworker who became disabled in an accident on the job, Solas fought discrimination wherever he found it. During the 1980s and 1990s, he filed dozens of lawsuits in his home state, winning again and again. "I just can't tolerate anyone getting ripped off of their freedoms," he explained. "We pay taxes just like everybody else and we should have the same entitlements." His actions dismayed many local officials and business leaders. But Solas was undaunted. "If they're having a hard time with it, then they're having a hard time with it," he stated. "Down the road they'll convert and understand that this was right. They'll realize they didn't understand it."

In their crusade for equal access, Greg Solas and other activists turn to a host of local, state, and federal laws that protect the civil rights of people with disabilities. Many of these laws grew out of the disability rights movement,

The modern American disability rights movement grew out of the rehabilitation movement that followed World War I, when thousands of U.S. servicemen returned home with war injuries.

which arose in the 1970s. Others date as far back as World War I. These changing laws reflect Americans' steady shift in attitudes toward people with disabilities.

During World War I, thousands of American servicemen received disabling wounds on the battlefield. Many more became disabled due to disease and malnutrition. After previous wars, the government had provided small pensions for disabled veterans. The veterans received money to compensate them for their injuries, but they received little help in rejoining the community. When the World War I veterans came home in 1918, a new movement was born. The "rehabilitation movement," as it came to be known, sought to retrain disabled veterans in the activities of daily living. It also encouraged them to learn skills that would help them find productive work. In the years following 1918, Congress passed laws that created the first rehabilitation programs in the country.

In 1935, Congress established Social Security, a federal program that continues today. Under this program, workers are required to pay part of their earnings into a special fund, from which they receive a steady pension after retirement. The Social Security program also provides financial assistance to people with disabilities who are below retirement age. In the mid-1930s, Social Security was the first federal program to offer benefits to nonveterans with disabilities.

The rehabilitation laws and the Social Security Act were intended to help people with disabilities to survive in society. Other early laws, however, were designed to protect society from people with disabilities. During the nineteenth and early twentieth centuries, most states passed "eugenics laws," which forbade people with mental retardation, epilepsy, and several other disabilities from marrying. In some states, people with these disabilities had to be sterilized—that is, they were forced to undergo operations so that they could not have children. Eugenics laws stemmed from the belief that disabling conditions were inherited from one's parents, and that people who had these conditions were a burden to the community.

Many other laws restricted the rights of people with disabilities. In some states, people who were blind or deaf were not permitted to teach in the public schools or to serve on juries. People with disabilities were automatically disqualified from holding civil service jobs; no matter how strong their qualifications might be, they could not pass the required medical examination.

Disabled people face three kinds of barriers—architectural, informational, and attitudinal—as they make their way in the world. Architectural barriers consist of curbs, stairs, narrow doorways, high counters, and other obstacles that hinder people with mobility impairments from traveling freely and using public facilities. People who are blind, deaf, or have learning disabilities must deal with informational barriers. Deaf people may need sign language interpreters at school, at work, or at the doctor's office. People who cannot read regular print need access to material in Braille or large print, or on audiotape. Like architectural barriers, informational barriers can keep people with disabilities from taking part in many activities.

Attitudinal barriers are the most difficult of all to remove. They come from society's long-held notion that people with disabilities are helpless and useless, and from a deep-seated fear of anyone who seems to be different. The negative attitudes of employers can keep a blind applicant from getting a job. The doubts and fears of a school principal may prevent a child with Down syndrome from attending a regular kindergarten.

In the long run, negative attitudes are responsible for most architectural and informational barriers. Until very recently, people with disabilities were not expected to take part in community life. Their needs rarely were considered when buildings were designed or programs were planned. Marilyn Phillips, a college professor who uses a wheelchair, summed it up: "I don't think it's fair for people to tell me, 'Why do you need a water fountain [that you can reach]? We'll get a drink for you.' Or, 'Why do you need a phone? We'll make the phone call for you.' 'Why do you need the fire alarms lowered? We can pull the alarms for you.' . . . What a world disabled people have been living in! Until you get disabled, you don't really know the score."

During the 1950s and 1960s, African-Americans fought for their civil rights in the United States. As they witnessed and sometimes aided in this struggle, many people with disabilities realized that they, too, were being treated as "separate and unequal." By the early 1970s, disabled people were busy changing the laws in California, New York, and many other states. They worked on city ordinances and state laws to eliminate architectural barriers and to combat discrimination in education and employment.

The first major breakthrough for people with disabilities came with the passage of the Rehabilitation Act of 1973. Section 504 was a small section added to the lengthy law almost as an afterthought. It stated, "No otherwise qualified handicapped individual . . . shall, solely by reason of his handicap, be excluded from participation in . . . any program or activity receiving federal financial assistance." Countless programs and activities received financial assistance from the federal government. They included hospitals, public transit, schools, parks, post offices, courthouses, libraries, and museums.

When disability rights activists read Section 504 of the Rehabilitation Act, they knew at once that they had been handed an extraordinary tool. Many businessmen and government officials feared the measure would be too costly and resisted putting the law into action. After disabled people lobbied and staged demonstrations, the regulations for Section 504 were finally signed into law in April 1977.

Another important federal law affecting people with disabilities was the Education for All Handicapped Children Act, passed in 1975. The law was passed because thousands of children with disabilities were being taught in segregated classes, or were not attending school at all. The new law mandated that children with disabilities must be educated in "the least restrictive setting possible." This law is now known as the Individuals with Disabilities Education Act (IDEA).

Despite the new laws, change did not come overnight. In 1989, a nationwide poll found that 59 percent of all people with disabilities were afraid to go out in public, dreading the stares and rejection of strangers. Architectural barriers kept 40 percent of the people surveyed from shopping, dining out, work-

Architectural barriers to buildings—such as stairs that lead to a front door—can be removed by installing wheelchair-accessible ramps.

Disability rights activists have found that they can spread their message to a large audience by staging public protests.

ing, or visiting friends. Nearly two-thirds of all disabled people of working age were unemployed; the majority wanted to work but could not find jobs.

On July 26, 1990, President George Bush signed a massive piece of civil rights legislation called the Americans with Disabilities Act (ADA). Some 180 organizations for and of people with disabilities worked together for the law's passage. The purpose of the ADA was "to provide a clear and comprehensive national mandate for the elimination of discrimination against individuals with disabilities." The law went much further than Section 504 of the Rehabilitation Act. It prohibited discrimination against people with disabilities in education, employment, transportation, telecommunications, public services, housing, and businesses.

At the signing ceremony, President Bush greeted Lisa Carl, a nineteen-year-old woman with cerebral palsy. Months before, Lisa had been refused admission to a Tacoma, Washington, movie theater. The owner had stated, "I

President George Bush signs the Americans with Disabilities Act into law in 1990. He is given a pen to sign the bill by Rev. Harold Wilke, a disability rights leader who has no arms.

don't want her in here, and I don't have to let her in." Now, as three thousand supporters cheered, President Bush shook Lisa's hand and declared, "Let the shameful wall of exclusion finally come tumbling down!"

The ADA is a "complaint driven" piece of legislation. People with disabilities must file lawsuits when they encounter discrimination, so the law can be enforced only by going to court. By 1995, some eleven thousand ADA lawsuits had been filed. The court process can be slow and expensive, and many people get discouraged. But activists like Greg Solas urge people to put the law to work. They warn that people with disabilities are too often afraid to ask for things that are theirs by right. "Nobody should be intimidated by the law," Solas says. "The laws were designed for people to use. If we use them, we can make things change."

O n the field, a representative from the St. Louis Browns held aloft a sign that read, SHOULD WE WALK HIM? In the stands, fans responded by raising signs that said either YES or NO. After quickly counting the votes, the manager signaled to his pitcher that the majority of the fans thought he should walk the next batter. The pitcher did just that.

It was Grandstand Managers Day in St. Louis, and the fans were calling the shots. Only one person could have been behind such a crazy stunt: Bill Veeck. Like all of Veeck's promotional events, Grandstand Managers Day was designed to entertain the people in the stands.

Bill Veeck spent most of his life in one ballpark or another. He was born on February 9, 1914, in Chicago, Illinois. His father, William Veeck Sr., was president of the Chicago Cubs. As a young boy, Bill accompanied his father to Wrigley Field to watch the Cubs play. Bill was only ten years old when he started counting tickets and selling food and souvenirs at the ballpark.

At age eighteen, Bill left Chicago to attend Kenyon College. During his second year at Kenyon, Bill's father died of leukemia. Since money was scarce, Bill left college to find work. He took a job in the Cubs' office at Wrigley Field.

Bill stayed with the Cubs for nearly eight years. During that time, he learned the fundamentals of running a baseball team. He also made his first mark in baseball history when he planted ivy at the base of the Wrigley Field outfield wall; today, the ivy-covered wall is one of the most famous and cherished sites in baseball.

In 1941, Bill left the Cubs to buy his own team. Using all but his very last dollar (which he framed and displayed) Bill Veeck bought the Milwaukee Brewers. At the time, the Brewers were a struggling minor-league team. Under Bill Veeck, they fought their way to first place, and Brewers fans were thrilled to have a winning team.

While in Milwaukee, Bill Veeck gained national attention for his pranks and publicity stunts. Since the United States was gearing up for World War II in the early 1940s, many factories were operating around the clock. When Bill realized that people who worked the night shift would miss night games, he introduced a special "Rosie the Riveter" morning game. The game began at 9:00 A.M., and any woman wearing a welding cap or riveting mask was admitted free of charge. The ushers, wearing pajamas and nightcaps, served breakfast in the stands.

After three seasons in Milwaukee, Bill joined the U.S. Marine Corps to fight in World War II. He returned from the war in 1945 with a severely wounded leg. In 1946, Veeck's right leg was amputated. But he handled this setback in the typical Veeck style—he threw a party to celebrate his new wooden prosthetic leg.

After losing his leg, Bill immediately went back to work in baseball. He bought the Cleveland Indians and began making headlines once again. In 1948, Veeck became the first American League owner to hire black players to play in the major leagues when he signed Larry Doby and Satchel Paige. The Indians were kings of baseball in 1948, winning the World Series, and putting Bill Veeck on top of the baseball industry. Still, Veeck moved on to new challenges. In 1949, he sold the Indians and bought the St. Louis Browns. While in St.

Bill Veeck at
Comiskey Park, Chicago

Louis, Bill literally lived in the ballpark. He and his wife, Mary Frances, occupied a small apartment in the Browns' stadium. The Browns were never a great team, but Bill managed to draw huge crowds to the stadium. Fans knew that something interesting would happen when Bill Veeck was running the show. Veeck said, "My philosophy as a baseball operator could not be more simple. It is to create the greatest enjoyment for the greatest number of people."

Veeck finally settled in Chicago when he bought the Chicago White Sox in 1959. He ran the team during the 1960s and 1970s. In the era under Veeck's ownership, Comiskey Park (the Sox home field) became known as the one ballpark in baseball where fans had as much fun in the stands as the players did on the field. Veeck installed a shower in the bleachers so fans could cool off on hot summer days. He even hired a barber to give haircuts to fans in the stands. And he was most famous for the Comiskey Park "exploding scoreboard." Whenever a Sox player hit a home run, sirens blared and the scoreboard glittered with flashing lights and pinwheels, while fireworks exploded overhead.

Bill Veeck retired from baseball in 1981. During his long career, he had owned and operated four different baseball teams. He had become a legend in baseball, a friend and ally to fans who saw most baseball owners as money-hungry. Bill Veeck went out of his way to make a ballgame an affordable and entertaining activity that an entire family could enjoy. Veeck was inducted into the Baseball Hall of Fame in 1991, five years after his death.

In the years after he retired, Bill Veeck continued to attend baseball games at Wrigley Field, the park where he grew up working with his father. On many summer days, he could be found in the bleachers, shirtless and laughing, elbow to elbow with his favorite people in the world—baseball fans. To reach the bleachers at Wrigley Field, Veeck had to climb a series of stairways and steep ramps. Though he had a variety of ailments and used a prosthetic leg, Veeck never complained or asked for assistance. He was just happy to be at home, in a ballpark. Veeck refused to allow his disability to limit his love of the game.

ALICIA ALONSO

1921–

Ballet Dancer

The daughter of a lieutenant in the Cuban army, Alicia Martinez enjoyed a life of privilege. A cook prepared the family's meals, gardeners tended the trees and flowers in the patios, and nursemaids cared for the four Martinez children. By the time she was four, Alicia showed an interest in dance. Later she recalled, "Mama used to put me in a room with a phonograph and a scarf. That would keep me quiet for a few hours, doing what I imagined was dancing."

Recognizing her talent, Alicia's parents enrolled her at the Sociedad pro Artes Musicales (Society for the Musical Arts) in Havana, Cuba. When she was ten, Alicia made her public debut, dancing in the Tchaikovsky ballet *Sleeping Beauty.*

At sixteen, Alicia married a fellow dancer, Fernando Alonso. The couple moved to New York City, where Alicia studied at the world-famous School of American Ballet. In 1939, Alicia went on tour with the American Ballet Caravan as a soloist. Later she signed with the American Ballet Theater. One of her first solo parts was that of the robin in Tchaikovsky's *Peter and the Wolf.*

Just as her career was gaining momentum, Alonso began to have serious problems with her vision. The retinas of both eyes became detached, leaving her totally blind. In the early 1940s, the treatment for detached retinas required absolute rest. For an entire year, Alonso was confined to bed, her eyes covered with bandages. Sandbags were piled around her to prevent her from shifting her position. Under no circumstances could she turn her head, laugh, or cry. The doctors warned her that any movement might jar loose the delicate retinas before they healed.

At first, this treatment tortured Alicia—movement had always been at the center of her life! But as time passed, she turned inward, living in the richness of her mind. Just before she lost her vision, she had begun to study the role of Giselle in the ballet by the same name. Now, as she lay in her nest of sandbags, she rehearsed the role inside her head. Day after day she practiced every glide and turn, each leap and bend and spin, until she knew the part to perfection.

The treatment did return some useful vision to Alonso, though her sight remained seriously limited. For the next several months, she worked to regain the muscle tone she had lost during a year without exercise. As she resumed her work on Giselle, she found that her mental rehearsals had paid off. She easily mastered the part, and it became the triumph of her career. From 1943 to 1946, she danced in *Giselle* with the American Ballet Theater. She also performed in such classical ballets as *The Nutcracker, Swan Lake,* and *Romeo and Juliet,* and in contemporary productions, including *Undertow* and *Fall River Legend.*

By now Alicia Alonso had a reputation among ballet enthusiasts throughout the world. Yet, though her future in the United States shone with promise, she longed for her native Cuba. She knew that aspiring young dancers in her native country had few opportunities, and she dreamed of finding a way to help them.

In 1948, Alicia and Fernando Alonso returned to Havana. With the help of Fernando's brother, they founded the Ballet Alicia Alonso, Cuba's first major ballet company. The company was a magnet for dancers from all over Latin America. To Alicia's dismay, however, few Cubans were qualified to join the

Alicia Alonso dances Swan Lake *in 1990, when she was 69 years old.*

troupe. The country did not offer proper training for talented young dancers. To meet this need, she established the Alicia Alonso Academy of Ballet in Havana. With her name behind it, the school drew some of the finest ballet instructors in the world. Suddenly ballet flourished in Cuba as it never had before.

During the early years, the ballet company and school received funding from the Cuban government under President Fulgencio Batista. But as time passed, money from the government dwindled. Most of the dancers were forced to take additional jobs in order to support themselves. They had less time and energy for ballet, and their work suffered. Because of money troubles, Alonso finally closed the school and the dance company, and she returned to the United States.

During the winter of 1957, Alonso spent ten weeks touring the Soviet Union, dancing in *Giselle* and *Swan Lake*. The United States and Soviet Russia were at the height of the Cold War, and Alonso was the first Western dancer to visit Communist Russia during these tense years.

In 1959, the Cuban government was overthrown by Fidel Castro's Communist troops. Thousands of upper-class Cubans fled to the United States, desperate to save their property and their lives. But Alicia Alonso decided to return to her homeland. She felt that the revolution offered hope for a better Cuban society, and she wanted to make a contribution. With $200,000 from Castro's new government, she reopened her ballet company and school as the Ballet Nacional de Cuba. She also established a network of smaller schools throughout the island nation. Alonso's fondest dreams were realized at last. "A rural child has an equal opportunity with a city child," she explained. "If there is dance talent, we will find it. If the child has a desire to dance, we will give him every chance to develop his talent."

The Ballet Nacional performed in schools, parks, and factories, bringing the grace and beauty of dance to Cuba's humblest citizens. It toured Latin America and visited the Soviet Union and the Communist nations of Eastern Europe. But for many years, the U.S. State Department forbade the ballet of Communist Cuba from performing in the United States. Alicia Alonso was an outcast from her adopted country.

During the late 1960s, Alicia Alonso's vision began to fail once more. Eventually she could distinguish only light from darkness. Undaunted, she continued to dance. She located her position with the help of bright spotlights and followed the voice of an assistant as she left the stage. She said that continuing to dance helped heal her, both in body and soul: "Dance works on the total being. By that I mean the mind and the spirit as well as the purely physical parts. I think of dance as the total antibiotic for healing."

In 1971, the Ballet Nacional was finally permitted to visit the United States, and Alonso danced as Giselle in New York. "In some respects the physical command is not so certain as it was years ago," wrote a dance critic in the *New York Times*. "But Alonso is now a far better dancer than she was. The nuances and grace notes that distinguish great classic dancing in the superbly accomplished are now very evident, and her musical phrasing is as individual as ever."

In 1972, Alonso traveled to Barcelona, Spain, where doctors again restored some useful vision. She continued to dance, to teach, and to choreograph new works for the Ballet Nacional. She was active with the World Council for Peace, using dance as a means to promote understanding between nations. In 1990, at the age of sixty-nine, she danced in *Swan Lake* for the fiftieth-anniversary gala of the American Ballet Theater.

Throughout her long career, Alicia Alonso has seen dance as a vehicle for personal fulfillment and for sharing with others. "I live when I dance," she says. "I live not just for myself. When I'm on stage with my dancers, I live with them. It is life."

ROY CAMPANELLA

1921–1993

Baseball Player

Roy Campanella was the child of an interracial marriage. His mother was African-American, and his father was an immigrant from Italy. Like millions of other families in the United States during the Great Depression of the 1930s, the Campanellas were hard-pressed for money. Roy's father made a meager living by peddling fruit and vegetables on the streets of Philadelphia. By the time Roy was nine years old, he was earning a quarter a day by helping his older brother deliver milk.

When he was a teenager, Roy showed unusual promise as an athlete. He won high-school letters in football, basketball, and track. But his greatest love was baseball, and he showed outstanding skill as a catcher. During his junior year, he began to play with a Philadelphia Negro League team, earning fifty dollars a weekend. Roy was so good at baseball that in 1937, he decided to drop out of high school and join another Negro League team, the Baltimore Elites.

For the first half of the twentieth century, African-Americans were not permitted to play baseball in the major leagues. Like Roy, countless talented black athletes were restricted to Negro League teams, where they earned far less money and achieved much less fame than they might in the all-white major leagues. But in 1947, baseball history was changed when Jackie Robinson joined the Brooklyn Dodgers. Dodgers owner Branch Rickey withstood the objections of every other team owner and signed Robinson to be the major leagues' first African-American player. As Robinson took baseball by storm and won the 1947 Rookie of the Year award, Branch Rickey continued to scout the Negro Leagues and sign other African-American stars, including Roy Campanella.

Campanella (or "Campy," as he was affectionately nicknamed) joined the Brooklyn Dodgers in the middle of the 1948 season and made an immediate impact. As an African-American catcher in a virtually all-white league, he had a difficult task. The catcher must communicate closely with the pitcher, as well as all of the players in the field. But Campy overcame many of his white teammates' (and opponents') racist and resentful attitudes. He quickly established himself as the best catcher in the National League, and a hitting star, as well. He won the league's Most Valuable Player award in 1951, 1953, and 1955. In ten years with the Dodgers, he hit 242 home runs, an average of 24 per season.

Roy Campanella was still at the peak of his career in the late 1950s. Then, on an icy night in January 1958, everything changed. Driving home to Long Island, New York, his car hit a patch of ice and skidded off the road. The accident broke Campanella's neck and damaged his spinal cord. It left him a quadriplegic, almost completely paralyzed from the neck down.

The news of Campanella's accident sent shock waves across the United States. The impact was felt not just among baseball fans, but by many people who knew nothing about sports. Some stunned fans mourned their hero as though he had died. But Roy Campanella was far from defeated. As he struggled to adjust to his disability, the nation's grief turned to admiration.

In 1958, most people with quadriplegia developed fatal medical complications. Fortunately, Campanella entered the Institute of Physical Medicine and Rehabilitation, a pioneering program created by Dr. Howard Rusk. The institute used the most advanced medical techniques to help patients reach their fullest physical potential. It also worked to instill confidence and hope, teaching patients

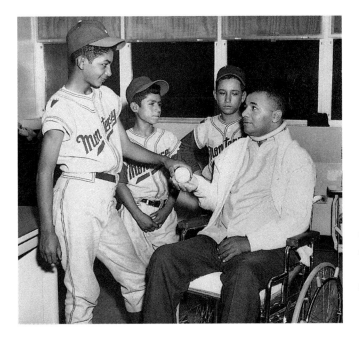

Both before and after his automobile accident, Roy Campanella was a hero to millions of children.

that they still could live rewarding lives with their disabilities. This is how Campanella explained his experience at the institute:

> *You go to school there. You go to two or three classes before lunch and two or three after. You learn how to adjust to the wheelchair, how to get in and out of cars, how to answer the telephone . . . how to use all the gadgets you need to write and eat with. And then there's the psychological thing. Paralyzed people can get so depressed. Thank goodness that part of it didn't bother me. When they put me in that wheelchair, I accepted it. For one thing, I was just happy to get out of bed. This chair is my freedom. It's the only thing in my life I can control.*

Two years after his accident, Campanella was dealt another severe blow. His wife, Ruth, left him, taking their three children. In 1964, Campanella remarried. His second wife, Roxie, remained his loyal supporter for the rest of his life.

Soon after he left the rehabilitation institute, Roy Campanella returned to the Dodgers as a spring-training instructor. With his long experience and keen understanding of baseball, he had a wealth of knowledge to share with young players. He described his work with enthusiasm: "I put on my baseball shirt and my cap, and I'm in this wheelchair and I'm going all over the place. I get out early and work with the catchers, even the veterans. I don't care how old you are, you'll see something in this game you've never seen before. I tell them what I've seen. . . . This is my life, you know."

While work with the Dodgers consumed much of Campanella's energy, he found time to help other people who were paralyzed due to spinal-cord injury. His story received so much publicity that people wrote to him from all over the world. He visited hospitals and spoke to community groups. Once, he and his wife took a newly paralyzed boy into their home. The boy had been refusing to cooperate with his doctors, but with Campanella's encouragement, the boy was soon able to feed himself and take a renewed interest in life.

Roy Campanella was elected into the National Baseball Hall of Fame in 1969. In 1978, the Dodgers (by then based in Los Angeles) offered him a position with the team's community relations department. Campanella loved dealing with the public, so he proved perfectly suited for the job. People were drawn to his warmth and his ready smile. One of his former teammates, Joe Black, recalled sending a friend to talk to Campy. "He came back saying, 'Why, that man just makes you feel so important! He makes you feel good all over!' That's what he did, all right. He just touched your life."

ROBERT DOLE

∽

1 9 2 3 –

Politician

D during the Great Depression, most American families struggled to earn enough money for food and shelter. The Doles of Russell, Kansas, were no exception. Robert Dole's father ran a distribution station for dairy products, and his mother traveled the country roads peddling sewing machines. After school, Robert delivered newspapers and worked at a drugstore soda fountain. To bring in a few more dollars, the Doles moved into the basement of their home and rented out the rooms upstairs. Robert's mother liked to tell the children, "Can't never did anything." It was a motto Robert Dole never forgot.

In 1941, Robert Dole entered the University of Kansas as a premed student. Shortly thereafter the United States entered World War II, and Dole was called up for military service in 1943. After two years in the army, he achieved the rank of second lieutenant. On April 14, 1945, he led an assault on a German stronghold in Italy's Po Valley. During the battle, an exploding shell fractured his spine, shattered his right shoulder, and left his body riddled with shrapnel. Doctors at the army hospital told him that he would never walk again.

Robert Dole spent the next three years in military hospitals and rehabilitation centers. At first, he was almost completely paralyzed. Gradually he regained movement in his legs, but most of the nerves in his right shoulder had been destroyed. When he finally returned home, he had only the most limited use of his right arm and hand.

Determined to complete his education, Dole enrolled at Washburn University in Topeka, Kansas. His focus had shifted from medicine to politics, and he earned a law degree from Washburn in 1951. That fall, he was elected to a two-year term as a representative in the Kansas legislature. In 1953, he became a prosecuting attorney for Russell County, a position he held for the next eight years.

Dole launched his career in national politics in 1960, when he won the Sixth Congressional District race in Kansas. He served in the U.S. House of Representatives for four terms, winning a reputation as a staunch conservative who opposed "spendthrift liberal legislation." During the John F. Kennedy and Lyndon Johnson presidencies, Dole took a firm stand against Medicare and federal antipoverty programs. Yet at the same time, he recognized the critical need for civil rights legislation. Dole supported the Civil Rights Act of 1964 and the Voting Rights Act of 1965.

Dole was elected to the U.S. Senate in 1968, where he proved a devoted champion of President Richard Nixon. The United States was enmeshed in a war in Vietnam, a conflict that had grown increasingly unpopular with the American people. As Nixon expanded the U.S. involvement in Southeast Asia, Dole was his unflagging supporter. He became known for his aggressive tactics on the Senate floor. The conservative Arizona senator Barry Goldwater once remarked, "He's the first man we've had around here in a long time who will grab the other side by the hair and drag them down."

President Nixon resigned in 1974, his reputation tarnished by the events known as the Watergate scandal. Though Dole was not involved in the scandal itself, in the public view, he was linked with Nixon. Nevertheless, he was reelected to his Senate seat by a narrow margin and remained a powerful force in Congress. At the 1976 Republican National Convention, President Gerald Ford chose Senator Dole as his running mate in his bid for reelection. The Republicans ultimately lost the election to Jimmy Carter.

During the 1980s, Dole's public image began to change. He supported the food stamps program and other legislation aimed at feeding the hungry. He also fought against many of Republican president Ronald Reagan's tax-slashing measures, fearing that they would threaten vital social programs. He also championed the Americans with Disabilities Act as it made its way through Congress. Dole sought to show the United States that conservative politics need not be "anti-people."

Dole became the leader of the Republicans in the U.S. Senate in 1984, a position he held until he resigned from the Senate on June 11, 1996. Dole left the Senate to devote himself full-time to running for president of the United States. In his farewell address to the Senate, he said, "The Bible tells us, 'To every thing there is a season.' Well, I think my season in the Senate is about to come to an end. But the new season before me makes this moment far less the closing of one chapter than the opening of another." Robert Dole was about to take on the greatest challenge of his political career—the race for the White House.

DANIEL INOUYE

1924–

U.S. Senator

Growing up in Honolulu, Hawaii, the four Inouye children knew two cultures. In public school, they spoke English and learned the history of Europe and the United States. In the special Japanese school they attended several hours a week, they learned the language and traditions of their parents' homeland. That sense of belonging to two cultures has been with Daniel Inouye throughout his life.

After graduating from high school in 1942, Inouye enrolled in a premed program at the University of Hawaii. In 1941, the United States had entered World War II, and most young men of college age were enlisting in the armed forces. In 1943, Inouye left his studies to join the army. He enlisted in the 442nd Combat Regiment, a unit composed of Nisei, or Japanese-Americans.

Because the United States was at war with Japan, Japanese-Americans were under suspicion by the U.S. government. Thousands had been stripped of their property and herded into special detention camps, despite the fact that they were American citizens.

The recruits of the 442nd were eager to prove that they were loyal Americans. They fought with remarkable courage through many fierce battles in Europe. The 442nd became the most highly decorated military unit in U.S. history.

In 1945, Daniel Inouye served with valor as a platoon leader in Italy's Po Valley. Two days before V-E Day (Victory in Europe Day, when the war in Europe ended), Inouye led the assault on a heavily defended German infantry division. In the heavy fighting, Inouye sustained serious wounds. He was shot in the stomach and in both legs, and a rifle grenade shattered his right arm. Nevertheless, he managed to rescue his platoon from enemy fire. For his heroism, Inouye was awarded the Distinguished Service Cross, the Bronze Star, and the Purple Heart.

The injuries to Inouye's right arm were so severe that it had to be amputated. He spent the next two years in army hospitals and rehabilitation centers, where he learned to eat, dress himself, and perform other everyday activities with only his left hand.

Inouye returned to the University of Hawaii in 1947. His career goal had shifted from medicine to law, and he majored in government and economics. He earned a law degree from George Washington University in 1952. While attending law school, Inouye became intrigued with the political scene in Washington, D.C. He volunteered to work with the Democratic National Committee and began learning the ins and outs of national politics.

In 1952, Daniel Inouye returned to Hawaii, which was still a U.S. territory. With a band of other Nisei war veterans, the young lawyer helped strengthen Hawaii's Democratic Party. Almost at once, Inouye became the party's rising star. In 1953, he was appointed to serve as an assistant prosecuting attorney for the city of Honolulu. The following year, he was elected to the Territorial House of Representatives. He became a member of the Territorial Senate in 1958. And when Hawaii became the nation's fiftieth state in 1959, Inouye ran for its first congressional seat. He won the election by a landslide and returned to Washington, D.C.

Daniel Inouye was the first Asian-American ever elected to the U.S.

Congress. In Washington, he championed civil rights legislation in the 1960s, and he often spoke out on behalf of Japanese-American citizens. In 1962, he was elected to the U.S. Senate, where he continued to forge his political career.

During his early years in the Senate, Inouye staunchly supported the policies of presidents John F. Kennedy and Lyndon Johnson. As a World War II veteran, he spoke in favor of the nation's military involvement in Vietnam. On more than one occasion, Inouye's name was listed among possible vice presidential candidates.

By the early 1970s, with President Richard Nixon in the White House, Inouye moved away from his pro–Vietnam War stand. He cosponsored the War Powers Act of 1973, which limited the president's ability to wage war without a formal declaration from Congress. The same year, he was appointed to the seven-member Senate Watergate Committee, which investigated President Nixon's alleged illegal activities during his 1972 reelection campaign. Inouye's colleagues and the general public were impressed by his integrity as he questioned witnesses during this shameful period in the nation's history.

In one election after another, the people of Hawaii gave Daniel Inouye their overwhelming support. Throughout his political career, Senator Inouye has earned a reputation for fairness, for a unique ability to bring opposing sides together. He is a skillful lawmaker who reviews every bill carefully before voting on it. He is a thoughtful, soft-spoken man whose Washington office reflects the exotic landscape of his home state. It is decorated with Hawaiian carvings, lush tropical plants, and a large aquarium.

Inouye married in 1949 and has one son, Daniel Jr. In his spare time, the senator enjoys gardening and playing the piano. He has mastered numerous classical pieces composed solely for the left hand. One of his favorite pastimes is playing pool, which he admits is much more enjoyable than attending Washington cocktail parties.

JOHN LANGSTON GWALTNEY

1928–

Anthropologist

W hen John Langston Gwaltney was a small boy, his parents discovered that his vision was failing. His mother knew he would need special education if he was to compete in society. But in the town of East Orange, just outside Newark, New Jersey, there were few opportunities for a blind African-American child. Unable to find a class for her son, John's mother wrote to the one person she was sure could help—Eleanor Roosevelt.

Eleanor Roosevelt, the wife of President Franklin D. Roosevelt, was revered throughout the nation as a champion of the poor. Her staff responded swiftly to Mrs. Gwaltney's letter, and things began to happen. Within a short time, John was enrolled in a special "sight-saving" class for blind and visually impaired children. In those days, it was believed that children with low vision could save their sight by using it sparingly. In a sight-saving class, teachers tried to help their students preserve their remaining sight.

John had already learned Braille from a blind social worker, but now his education began in earnest. He loved to read. But at times books gave him only the vaguest notions about the real world. One day when he was eight years old, he asked his mother what a pig was like. He had read about pigs in stories, but he had never had the chance to touch one. John's mother, who had grown up on a farm in Virginia, was appalled by this gap in his education. As soon as she could, she took him to visit a farm, where he got hands-on experience with pigs, cows, chickens, and an assortment of other animals.

As part of her campaign to broaden John's world, his mother sent him to a camp for blind children in the hills of northern New Jersey. At Camp High Point, he swam, rowed, and hiked. He also met children and counselors from all over the state, people from every level of society. He loved to observe the people around him, trying to understand how they thought and why they behaved as they did.

John's parents were aware of only two professions open to blind people—begging and the ministry. His mother encouraged John to consider a career in the church. But at the age of nine, John concluded that he did not want to be a minister. The more he explored such subjects as science and history, the less he could accept the Bible as literal truth. He wanted to use his powers of reason to learn about the world through study and firsthand experience.

John Gwaltney was the first blind student to attend his local high school. Since few of his textbooks were available in Braille, he depended on volunteer readers. John was among the top students in his class. When he graduated, a generous benefactor offered to finance his studies at either Cambridge or Oxford University in England. But John's mother had become seriously ill, and he felt that he should stay close to home. He attended Upsala, a small, liberal arts college in East Orange, where he majored in history.

After he earned his B.A. degree, John Gwaltney taught classes for adults at the Henry George School in New York City. Determined to continue his studies, he enrolled in a doctoral program in history at Columbia University. He planned to do research on the North African military slave trade—the practice of selling slaves to serve as soldiers. After two years, however, he encountered a major roadblock. A leading professor in the history department insisted that John never would find a job, even if he received his Ph.D. The professor pointed out that some of his own former students—white, sighted, and highly qualified—could not find work in their field. John had two strikes against him: his race and his disability. The professor was convinced that John could not succeed as a scholar and refused to authorize him for further coursework. Despite strong recommendations from other members of the faculty, John Gwaltney was forced to leave the history program.

For a time, Gwaltney was devastated. Two years of hard work had been swept aside by one man's prejudice. He had wanted to teach history at a university, but now he had to seek a new direction for his life.

That direction became clear when a friend from Columbia introduced him to the world-famous anthropologist Margaret Mead. Mead was a highly respected professor at Columbia and the author of many groundbreaking books. Without hesitation, she accepted Gwaltney as a doctoral candidate. He was enthralled by anthropology, the study of human cultures. The field allowed him to explore some of the questions that had fascinated him most of his life: How did minority groups keep their cultures alive despite oppression by the social majority? How did individuals find the courage to defy conventions and stand up for what they believed was right?

In order to earn his degree, Gwaltney had to conduct original research. Margaret Mead suggested that he study the effects of river blindness among the Chinantec Indians of southeastern Mexico. River blindness, or onchocerciasis, is a parasitic disease carried by flies in many tropical regions. Among the Chinantec in the Mexican state of Oaxaca, the incidence of river blindness was very high. How were blind people perceived in a Chinantec village? How did this tribal culture deal with its blind members?

With Margaret Mead's help, Gwaltney obtained a research grant through the National Institutes of Health (NIH). In 1963, he set out with a student assistant to find the village of San Pedro Yolox. They rode as far as buses would carry them, and then hiked up the rugged mountain slopes to the village. As they had planned, the assistant departed within a few days. John Gwaltney was on his own.

The Chinantec agreed to let Gwaltney live in their village, but they were suspicious of this blind, bearded stranger. Unlike the blind people of the village, he walked freely and confidently, using nothing more than a metal cane to guide him. Gwaltney knew Spanish, as did many of the Chinantec. But Spanish was the language of the Mexican army and of the wealthy ranchers who were forever trying to seize the Indians' land. Some people thought Gwaltney might be a spy, prying into their secrets. One old woman declared that his cane had magical powers. She insisted it could turn people into pigs, which would be sent to the United States for butchering. Few of the villagers believed her, and Gwaltney slowly won the people's trust. Little by little he learned about their beliefs and came to understand their view of the world. But as he reflected later, "When they don't want you to know something, the Chinantec can devise dozens of ways to keep it from you."

In August 1963, some two hundred thousand people gathered in Washington, D.C., to march with Dr. Martin Luther King Jr. for civil rights. Before he left for Mexico, Gwaltney had promised to organize a march in Mexico City to support the issue of civil rights in Mexico. As Gwaltney explains, "A promise freely given is something which our people take very seriously." When the time approached, he left San Pedro Yolox and contacted all the Americans he knew in Mexico. Many people, both black and white, agreed to join him in the march. But on the appointed day, none of them appeared. John Gwaltney was alone on the Paseo de la Reforma, Mexico City's main boulevard, with his placards and a police escort. He marched for several blocks, until the chief of police appeared and demanded his permit. He did not have the proper papers to lead a march, he was informed coldly. For a few hours, Gwaltney feared he might be in serious trouble. When he finally was released from police custody, he hurried back to the safety of the mountains, satisfied that he had kept his promise.

After a year in Mexico, John Gwaltney returned to Columbia, earning his Ph.D. in anthropology in 1967. That year his paper on river blindness was one of two to receive Columbia's prestigious Ansley Dissertation Award. Dr. Gwaltney recounted his experiences among the Chinantec in a book entitled *Thrice Shy*.

Dr. John Gwaltney taught at Courtland State College in upstate New York for four years. In 1971, he became professor of anthropology at Syracuse University, where he spent the rest of his teaching career. As an offshoot of his anthropological studies, he became an oral historian, gathering first-person accounts of people's lives. His book *Drylongso* brings together the oral histories of some fifty African-American men and women from a wide variety of backgrounds. In *The Dissenters*, he interviews people who dared to break with conventions in order to uphold their beliefs. In his work, he received ongoing support from his wife, Judy, and his research assistant, James Yohannan.

Many of John Gwaltney's friends and relatives call him by his middle name, Langston. But to those closest to him in the African-American community, he is known as Rigo. The name *Rigo* is an African word meaning "ritual carver." As a young man, Dr. Gwaltney learned the art of carving masks and other sacred objects of wood and stone. Long ago these objects were central to the religious practices of many African peoples. Despite slavery and Christianity, the tradition of the carvings still survives. Gwaltney was carefully taught by nine elders of the community. They also instructed him in the responsibilities that go along with the carver's position. In his turn, he has passed the carver's art on to others, keeping alive an ancient tradition that has endured the extremes of adversity.

CHRISTY BROWN

1932–1981

Writer

"He's a hopeless case," the doctors told Christy Brown's mother. "There are institutions for children like that." But Mrs. Brown refused to listen. Her three-year-old son could not sit up, crawl, or speak. But she was convinced that he understood everything around him, that his mind was aware of the world.

Christy Brown was born in Dublin, Ireland. He was the tenth in a family of twenty-two children, thirteen of whom survived to adulthood. Christy's birth was difficult, and for a few minutes the new baby did not breathe. The lack of oxygen damaged Christy's brain, causing a condition called athetoid cerebral palsy. Christy had almost no control over his muscles, which twitched and jerked constantly. "I seemed to be convulsed with movement—wild, stiff, snake-like movement that never left me except in sleep," he wrote years later in his autobiography. "My fingers twisted and twitched continually, my arms twined backwards and would often shoot out suddenly this way and that, and my head lolled and sagged sideways. I was a queer, crooked little fellow."

Busy as she was, Christy's mother found time every day to work with him. She showed him pictures, read him stories, and made sure he was always in the midst of the family's activities. He lay on the kitchen floor near the fire, surrounded by noisy, laughing brothers and sisters, unable to tell them his thoughts.

One December afternoon when Christy was five years old, he watched his sister writing on a slate with a piece of yellow chalk. Suddenly he reached out with his left foot, seized the chalk between his toes, and drew a mark across the brick floor. The family stared in amazement. Realizing that this might be the breakthrough she longed for, Christy's mother knelt beside him. She drew the letter A on the floor, and urged him to copy it. In his autobiography, Christy Brown remembered the scene that changed his life: "I shook, I sweated and strained every muscle, my hands were so tightly clenched that my fingernails bit into the flesh. . . . But I drew it, the letter A. There it was on the floor before me—shaky, with awkward, wobbly sides and a very uneven central line, but it was the letter A. . . . That one letter scrawled on the floor with a bit of yellow chalk gripped between my toes was my road to a new world, my key to mental freedom."

By the time he was seven, Christy had learned to read and could write by holding a chalk or pencil with his left foot. His left leg and foot were the only parts of his body he could control. He never wore shoes. If anyone made him put shoes on, he felt the way most people do when their hands are tied.

With much effort, Christy learned to speak, though few people outside his family could understand him. He also discovered that he could scoot across the floor on his bottom, pushing himself with his left leg. Riding in a rattly go-cart nicknamed Henry, he went with his brothers on picnics and trips to the canal. Sometimes he tumbled out when the cart hit a bump, but Christy learned to fall without getting hurt. He was one of the boys, full of mischief, eager for each new adventure.

Then, when Christy was ten years old, one of Henry's axles broke. The go-cart could not be fixed. Every day Christy sat in the yard, watching his brothers set off without him. He felt abandoned, an outcast, different from everyone else.

He grew to hate his body and the suffering it was causing him. He despised "the sight of [my] hands, the sight of my wobbly head and lopsided mouth when I saw them in the mirror." When his mother bought him a proper wheelchair, Christy refused to go out with the boys again. Unwilling to face the stares of strangers, he remained at home, isolated and lonely.

Christy emerged from his depression when he discovered that he could paint. Holding a paintbrush with his toes, Christy painted on paper that his mother or father tacked to the floor so it wouldn't slide away. Christy copied pictures from books or painted scenes he remembered from the Dublin streets. He worked alone, day after day. "I had a feeling of pure joy as I painted, a feeling I had never experienced before and which seemed almost to lift me above myself."

As the years passed, Christy's older brothers and sisters married and moved away. His own life had no direction. He had no plans, no hope for his future. When he was eighteen, he met Dr. Robert Collis, an expert on cerebral palsy, who had just opened a new clinic in Dublin. He had seen Christy years ago, when his brother Jim carried him on his back to a movie. Now the doctor had tracked Christy down to offer him a new treatment—physical therapy. Dr. Collis's visit seemed like the answer to Christy's prayers.

The doctors at the clinic offered Christy Brown the hope for greater movement and clearer speech. But they required a terrible sacrifice. They insisted that he must stop using his left foot for writing and painting. The excessive use of his foot caused undue strain to the rest of his body. Besides, they argued, as long as he could use his foot, he never would work to develop his hands. He never would be able to live a "normal" life.

For the next three years, Christy Brown went to the clinic every morning. The rigorous exercise program gave him new control over his body. He learned to stand and even to walk short distances. He learned breathing techniques that helped him to speak more clearly. But he gained little use of his hands. He yearned for the freedom he once knew when he could paint and write. At last,

Christy Brown became a famous author by writing with his left foot.

in a moment of frustration, he kicked off his shoe and began to write with his foot again. Writing with his foot was not considered "normal" in society, but it worked for him. "I felt a different person," he later recalled. "I wasn't unhappy anymore. I didn't feel frustrated or shut up any more. I was free. I could think. I could live. I could create."

Soon after he met Dr. Collis, Christy Brown decided to write his life story, and in 1954, Brown published his autobiography, *My Left Foot*. The book was an instant success in Ireland and was published in fifteen other countries. Years later, Brown described *My Left Foot* as "the kind of book they expected a cripple to write, too sentimental and corny."

Through the decades that followed, Brown continued to develop as a painter and a writer. He learned to use an electric typewriter, which he could operate easily even with his hands' limited movement. In 1970, he published his first novel, *Down All the Days*. Drawing upon his childhood memories, it is the story of a boy with cerebral palsy growing up on the streets of Dublin. Though he is unable to speak, the boy is a keen observer of the people around him. Brown published two more novels during his lifetime, *A Shadow on Summer* and *Wild Grow the Lilies*. He also completed three books of poetry.

In 1972, Brown married Mary Carr, a former nurse. At first, his family opposed the marriage, afraid that Mary was interested only in his money and fame. But the marriage proved to be a happy one. Because of his problems with muscle control, Christy always needed assistance with his personal care. A family member or hired assistant helped him with dressing, going to the bathroom, and eating. He also experienced difficulty in swallowing, which led to his death. In 1981, at the age of forty-nine, Christy choked to death on some food. His last novel, *A Promising Career*, was published after his death. Although his life was a relatively short one, Christy Brown packed the years with experience and saw the world with the reflective gaze of the true artist.

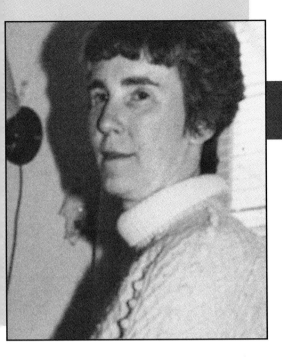

BEVERLY BUTLER

1932–

Writer

As she was growing up in Milwaukee, Wisconsin, Beverly Butler displayed an active imagination. She liked to draw and color. Best of all, she loved to spin wild fantasies for her younger brother. Her grandmother always said that she was a born storyteller. Beverly reflects, "I think that was because she didn't quite believe half the things I told her."

Beverly was born with cataracts on both eyes. A cataract is a thin, cloudy membrane that can limit a person's vision. When she was thirteen, she also developed a painful eye condition called glaucoma. Doctors tried to save her sight with surgery, but the operation was a disaster. It destroyed the remaining sight in one eye, and the other eye deteriorated rapidly as well. Within a few weeks, Beverly was totally blind.

For Beverly, the worst thing about losing her sight was the way people treated her. Most of her old friends suddenly disappeared. The few who dropped in to visit seemed to feel awkward and found excuses to leave early. Her parents hoped that her blindness would be temporary. They waited and waited, but her vision did not return. To help pass the time while she was out of school, her father got her some books about Braille from the library. Together they learned the Braille system for reading and writing by touch.

After several months at home, Beverly Butler entered the Wisconsin School for the Blind at Jaynesville. It was a residential school, where the students lived in dormitories on the campus. Beverly soon realized that the teachers expected very little of their blind students. They seemed convinced that children who couldn't see never would amount to anything. Instead of science and history, the students were taught broom making and chair caning. Beverly tried to be as uncooperative as possible, hoping that she would be expelled so she could go home. But it was hard to get into trouble when no one expected her to do well in the first place.

Beverly begged her parents to let her enroll in her neighborhood school back in Milwaukee. At first, they encouraged her to give the school a chance. Eventually, however, they recognized how unhappy she was and understood that the school in Jaynesville would not help her to live a normal life. But the Milwaukee public schools said that a blind student did not belong in the regular classroom. Beverly's father fought a long battle with the school board. Finally Beverly was accepted on a trial basis. She could stay in the public school as long as there weren't any problems.

Under tremendous pressure to succeed, Beverly became a straight-A student for the first time in her life. Her parents and some of her classmates read her textbooks to her, and she took notes in Braille. Many of the students became her close friends. She learned to touch-type so that her teachers could read her test papers and written work.

To ease her boredom at the school for the blind, Beverly had begun writing stories. She continued to write during high school, though she never showed her stories to her teachers. Somehow she suspected that anything that was so much fun had to be against the rules. Nevertheless, she made up her mind that writing would be her life's work. Friends and teachers were skeptical. It was hard enough for a sighted person to become a professional writer, they pointed out. How could a blind person compete?

Beverly refused to be discouraged. She was thrilled to discover that Mount Mary College in Milwaukee offered several creative writing courses. Furthermore, Mount Mary was only two blocks from her home. She'd had enough of dormitory living to last her a lifetime.

At Mount Mary, Beverly Butler enrolled in a course on novel writing. Again and again the professor told the students to "write about what you know." Since she had lived there all her life, Beverly decided to use Wisconsin as her setting. But instead of describing modern situations, she chose to write about Wisconsin's early French and English settlers. Her first book, a young-adult novel called *Song of the Voyageurs*, was published in 1955, the year after she received her B.A. degree.

With a published novel to her credit, Beverly found that people suddenly took her seriously as a writer. She wrote three more historical novels and earned an M.A. in literature from Marquette University, sponsored by a Woodrow Wilson Fellowship.

As a college student, Beverly Butler once tried to write a novel about a girl who was blind. She hated the book so much that she stuffed the whole manuscript, page by page, into the fireplace. But for years, her editor kept pushing her to write about a blind character. She refused to consider the idea again. If she wrote about someone who was blind, people might believe that she couldn't write about anything else. She did not want to be categorized as a blind writer who wrote about nothing but blindness.

Then one day, lost in thought on a long bus ride, she realized that her own experiences could grow into a book she would like to write. Drawing on her days at the Wisconsin School for the Blind and her return to public school, she wrote *Light a Single Candle*, which was published in 1964. "Writing that book was a real catharsis for me," she explains. "I think for the first time I really came to terms with the fact that I was blind."

To her surprise, *Light a Single Candle* outsold any of Beverly's other books. She was dismayed that so many readers were intrigued by what she regarded as the boring facts of blindness—ordinary details about dressing, doing school-work, and getting around. She was delighted, however, when she heard that the book was banned at the Wisconsin School for the Blind. According to rumor, students smuggled it in and read it secretly.

During the 1960s, Beverly Butler taught at Mount Mary College while continuing to write. In 1974, she married a writer named Ted Olsen and moved to northern Wisconsin. Beverly and Ted never wrote a book together, but they supported and critiqued each other's work. Beverly Butler continued to write historical novels for young-adult fiction readers. She also ventured into the occult with her books *Ghost Cat* and *Witch's Fire*. In a nonfiction book, *Maggie by My Side*, she described life with a dog guide.

After her husband's death in 1993, friends urged Beverly to move back to Milwaukee, where she would not be so isolated. But she lived a mile down the road from the nearest town and had grown to love the quiet of the woods. "I like the sense of space," she says. "I like to step outside and hear nothing but birdsong. It really isn't lonely. The winters up here are so long that neighbors make a big effort to get together."

Most of Beverly Butler's novels are about independent, willful girls growing up in a time long before anyone had heard of women's liberation. Beverly has shown much of the same pioneering spirit in her own life. From the time she decided to attend regular school, she has been breaking new ground, opening roads for others to follow.

AUDRE LORDE

1934–1992

Poet, Activist

When Audre Lorde's parents moved to New York City from the Caribbean island of Grenada, they thought they would stay for only a few years. They would work hard, save money, and go back to start a new life on the island. But during the 1930s, a massive economic depression engulfed the United States. Jobs were scarce. Day-to-day survival became a struggle. It was impossible for the family to save money, and the island of Grenada became a faraway dream.

Audre Lorde grew up listening to her parents' stories of the island she had never seen. Sometimes she felt like a foreigner on the streets of her Harlem neighborhood, as if she had been uprooted from her true home. In other ways, too, she felt separate from the people around her. She was overweight, she was very nearsighted, and she loved to write poetry. Wherever she went, she never quite seemed to fit in.

When Audre was in high school, some of her teachers encouraged her to write. One of her poems was accepted by *Seventeen* magazine and appeared in 1951. After graduation, Audre rented her own apartment and enrolled at Hunter College. She took breaks from college several times in order to work and travel, but she finally earned her B.A. in 1959. The following year she received a master's degree in library science from Columbia University. For several years, she worked as a librarian.

Audre married in 1960 and had two children, Beth and Jonathan. She continued writing poetry, publishing frequently in literary magazines. Her first book of poems, *The First Cities*, appeared in 1968. That same year she spent six weeks as writer in residence at Tougaloo College in Mississippi. At Tougaloo, she met a woman named Frances Clayton, who became her lifelong partner. Audre Lorde's marriage ended in 1970. In 1971, she publicly declared that she was a lesbian. She taught creative writing at City College of New York and conducted a course on racism in America at John Jay College of Criminal Justice. Her poetry gained wider recognition, and she traveled around the country, giving lectures and readings. In 1974, Lorde's collection of poems, *From a Land Where Other People Live*, was nominated for the prestigious National Book Award.

In her lectures and writing, Audre Lorde spoke out for the oppressed—for women, for gays and lesbians, for people of racial minorities. She described herself boldly as "a black Lesbian feminist warrior poet mother." Without apology, she presented each part of her identity to the world.

In 1978, Audre Lorde published *The Black Unicorn*, one of her best-known books of poetry. It was also in 1978 that she discovered a small lump in her right breast. The lump proved to be cancerous. To save her life, her breast was removed in an operation called a mastectomy.

At first, Audre Lorde was grief stricken by the loss of her breast. But as the days passed, she knew she must accept the change in her body. To her dismay, nurses urged her to wear an artificial breast, or prosthesis, tucked into her bra. People kept assuring her that with the prosthesis she would look "normal"; no one would ever know the difference. Audre Lorde felt there was something deeply wrong with such thinking. It pressured her to hide from the truth of her own experience. "Not even the most skillful prosthesis in the world could undo

[my] reality, or feel the way my breast had felt," she wrote in her journal. "Either I love my body one-breasted now, or remain forever alien to myself." Audre Lorde never wore a prosthesis.

Her treatment for cancer prompted Audre to examine many issues in American health care. She concluded that hospitals often urged treatments that were unnecessary or even dangerous. They did this because they needed to make money, and certain surgical procedures were very profitable. At the same time, potentially valuable alternative treatments were being suppressed. In her book *The Cancer Journals*, Lorde explored both the emotional and political aspects of having cancer.

After her mastectomy, Audre Lorde resumed her writing, teaching, and lecturing. But she was keenly aware that her life might be shorter than she once had expected. In essays and poems, she explained that her awareness of death helped her to live as fully as possible.

In 1984, Audre Lorde was diagnosed with liver cancer. This time, she refused conventional treatment. After extensive research, she underwent an experimental treatment in Germany. Three years later, her cancer returned once again.

In order to get well, Audre Lorde decided she must radically change the way she lived her life. To escape the stress of New York City, she moved to St. Croix in the U.S. Virgin Islands. She ate wholesome foods, exercised, and practiced meditation. Audre Lorde outlived the doctors' predictions by many years. She recounted her ongoing struggle with cancer in her book *A Burst of Light*, which won the American Book Award in 1989.

During her lifetime, Audre Lorde published nine collections of poetry, an autobiography, and several collections of essays. A final book of poems appeared after her death. She received honorary doctorate degrees from Oberlin and Haverford Colleges and was selected as poet laureate by the State of New York in 1991.

Audre Lorde's work reflects her lifelong battle against prejudice in all its forms. She often pointed out that all of us at times behave oppressively toward others. Throughout her life, Lorde worked to unmask injustice wherever she found it. The first, most crucial step was to break silence. As she put it, "Silence has never brought us anything of worth."

ED ROBERTS

1939–1995

Disability Rights Activist

There was nothing more to be done, the doctors told twenty-nine-year-old Rus Cooper. She was permanently disabled. On Monday, an ambulance would carry her from the hospital to a nursing home, where she would spend the rest of her life. Rus Cooper lay in her hospital bed, too depressed to care what happened around her. But suddenly, through the chatter coming from her television, she caught the words "independent living for people with disabilities." A news program was interviewing a man named Ed Roberts, a quadriplegic who used a motorized wheelchair. As Rus Cooper listened, enthralled, Roberts spoke of a rising movement among disabled people. He talked about people with disabilities fighting to take control of their lives.

When the ambulance arrived the next morning, Rus Cooper refused to go to the nursing home. Instead she contacted Ed Roberts, who helped her arrange to return home. Eventually Rus married, had two children, and became an ordained minister. Like thousands of other people with disabilities, she believed that Ed Roberts had transformed her life.

As a boy in Burlingame, California, Ed Roberts fell in love with baseball. He dreamed of someday playing on a professional team. But when he was four-

Ed Roberts
127

teen, he contracted poliomyelitis. His fever soared, and his muscles became paralyzed almost overnight. He lost all movement in his legs, torso, arms, and hands—with the exception of two fingers. He could not even breathe without the aid of a machine called an iron lung. "You should hope he dies," a doctor told Ed's mother. "If he lives, he'll be no more than a vegetable for the rest of his life."

Convinced that he had nothing to look forward to, Ed tried to starve himself to death. Day after day he refused to eat, until his weight dropped to fifty pounds. The nurses then force-fed him through a tube, depriving him of even this last shred of control.

One day Ed's private-duty nurse quit. Suddenly he found himself alone on the hospital ward. No one stood beside his bed, managing his life. For the first time since his illness, Ed Roberts found that he wanted to live, to take charge of his own future. Years later he remarked, "I decided that if I was destined to be a vegetable, I'd be an artichoke. Prickly on the outside, but with a big heart."

For three years, Ed was a homebound student, taking part in high-school classes by means of a telephone hookup. He threw all of his energy into his studies. By his senior year, Ed needed the iron lung only at night, and his parents persuaded the school to let him attend regular classes. The other students stared as his brother pushed Ed's wheelchair into the building on his first morning. But Ed realized that stares couldn't hurt him. If people were going to make him the center of attention, he might as well think of himself as a star.

Ed Roberts was an A student during his senior year. As commencement approached, however, the principal announced that Ed would not be allowed to graduate. Because of his disability, he had not taken the required physical education courses. When the principal would not reconsider, Ed and his parents argued their case before the school board. The board agreed that the principal was being unfair, and Ed graduated with his class. "My parents were wonderful advocates," Ed remembered. "They taught me my first lessons about political protest."

After two years at a community college, Ed Roberts decided he wanted to attend the University of California at Berkeley. But the university refused to admit him. "We've tried cripples before," he was told, "and they just don't work out." Eventually, he persuaded the university to accept him on a trial basis. He was a pioneer, the first quadriplegic ever to enroll at Berkeley.

Few of the buildings on the Berkeley campus were accessible to a person who used a wheelchair. Ed Roberts could not even live in one of the regular dormitories. Instead, he had to live at Cowell Hospital on the university grounds. Despite these obstacles, he did well in all of his classes. He was so successful that the university admitted several more disabled students over the next few years. By the time Ed was a senior, eight or nine students were living at the hospital and relishing the excitement of college life. They studied, went to parties, and lounged on the grass. They called themselves the "Rolling Quads."

The 1960s was a time of widespread political activism on college campuses. Berkeley stood at the hub of the movement against the war in Vietnam. Ed Roberts and the other disabled students attended rallies, joined marches, and wrote fiery articles for the campus paper. Roberts realized that the tactics of protest could be used by people with disabilities to bring about much-needed changes.

Many of the disabled students at Berkeley had serious problems with the Department of Vocational Rehabilitation (DVR). The DVR was supposed to provide counseling and financial aid that would help disabled people reach their educational and career goals. But the counselor assigned to the Berkeley students had no faith in these students' abilities. Instead of providing encouragement, she threatened and harassed them. By withdrawing money that rehabilitation had agreed to pay them for living expenses, she forced several of the students to leave school. At first, Ed Roberts tried to negotiate with the DVR. When nothing changed, he turned to the local media. The papers ran a powerful story about disabled students thwarted in their quest for an education. Within weeks, all of the Rolling Quads were back on campus.

With several other disabled students, Ed Roberts gathered local resources for people with disabilities. He helped create a list of wheelchair-accessible apartments and collected the names of people willing to work as personal-care assistants. The students organized a workshop to repair wheelchairs quickly and efficiently. They also began to do peer counseling, sharing their experiences with others to help in solving problems.

Ed Roberts earned a B.A. and a master's degree in political science from Berkeley. He entered a Ph.D. program and completed all of the requirements for his doctorate except the dissertation. For several years, he served as a teaching assistant at Berkeley. Later he taught political science at Nairobi College, a small college for students of racial minorities. In 1969, Roberts was invited to act as consultant to the Special Students Program within the U.S. Office of Education in Washington, D.C. The Office of Education was developing a pilot program for minority students. Roberts wrote the guidelines with reference to students with disabilities.

In 1972, Roberts obtained federal funding to start a model program in Berkeley for people with disabilities. It was called the Center for Independent Living (CIL), and it embodied the philosophy that he had been evolving ever since he became disabled. Roberts believed that people with disabilities must gain control over their own lives. For too long, they had been pushed into the background while doctors, social workers, and other professionals spoke for them. At the Center for Independent Living, Roberts showed people with disabilities how to speak on their own behalf. Housing lists, wheelchair repair, and peer counseling were part of the program, just as they had been at the university. But he also encouraged disabled people to see themselves as a force in the political arena. By pressuring lawmakers through negotiations, publicity, and protest, they could make their presence felt at every level of government. They could push for changes that would bring disabled people into the American mainstream. Sometimes people complained to Roberts that they hated politics and didn't want to get involved. He responded, "Get political or die, or go to a

Ed Roberts

nursing home. If you're not part of the political process, people will be talking for you."

In 1975, Governor Jerry Brown appointed Ed Roberts to serve as director of the California Department of Vocational Rehabilitation. As a student at Berkeley, Roberts had led protests against the DVR's policies. Now he headed the agency, in charge of more than two thousand employees. In his work at DVR, he strove to implement policies that would empower rehabilitation clients.

In 1984, Ed Roberts was selected to receive a "genius award" from the MacArthur Foundation. The MacArthur Fellowships are awarded each year to women and men who have made extraordinary contributions to society. In the course of the following five years, Roberts received $225,000 to help him carry on his work. He used much of this money to establish the World Institute on Disability (WID). Based in Oakland, California, WID brings together experts on every aspect of disability to help formulate social policy. The organization examines disability-related issues in health care, education, employment, housing, transportation, and many other areas. Ed Roberts served as president of

WID until his death from a heart attack in 1995.

Ed Roberts's death touched people all over the world. Letters from grieving friends and admirers poured into WID headquarters. Among Roberts's longtime supporters was President Bill Clinton. Clinton captured the feelings of thousands of others when he said, "As an international leader and educator in the independent living and disability rights movements, he fought throughout his life to enable all persons with disabilities to fully participate in mainstream society. Mr. Roberts was truly a pioneer. His vision and ability to bring people together should be an example for all Americans."

H enry Kisor, known to his family as "Hank," was born on August 17, 1940, in Midland Park, New Jersey. At a very early age, Henry showed signs of having a talent for language. His mother recalls that during a long drive to Florida, her precocious two-year-old son entertained her by singing every word of "The Eyes of Texas Are Upon You." This gift for language was to prove exceptionally important to Henry Kisor's future.

During World War II, Manoun Kisor, Henry's father, entered the navy as a Supply Corps lieutenant. The family moved from New Jersey to the Fort Lauderdale Naval Air Station. While the Kisors were living in Florida, Henry, their youngest son, developed a bad fever. The navy doctors were not sure whether Henry had meningitis, encephalitis, or both. For nearly nine days, the boy was so ill that they were afraid he would die. When at last he began to recover, the doctors told his parents that the fever had destroyed his auditory nerves. Three-year-old Henry Kisor was completely deaf.

As Manoun and Judith Kisor struggled to accept this fact, they were faced with some very difficult choices. How were they going to educate their son? In 1944, the options available to the parents of a deaf child were very limited. At that time, few cities offered educational programs for deaf children. The programs that did exist separated the deaf children from children who could hear. In many states, deaf children were sent to residential schools. Henry's parents refused to send him away. Instead, they decided to work with their son at home.

In the first months after losing his hearing, Henry learned to read lips when people spoke to him in simple terms. He could not follow anything complicated, however, and he often grew frustrated. Because he could no longer hear others speak, or even hear his own words, Henry soon stopped talking. His parents were afraid he would forget everything he had learned about speech and language.

Fortunately, Judith Kisor happened to see an advertisement for the Mirrielees system, a new way to teach deaf children. The system had been created by Doris Irene Mirrielees. She believed that deaf children could lead full and productive lives if they were given the key to understanding language. The key was learning to relate everyday experiences to written words.

Using the Mirrielees system, the Kisors began teaching their son to read. They led him on small adventures, and afterwards they showed him words and pictures that described the things he had done and seen. Soon Henry began to recognize the connection between objects and experiences and the words that represented them. Judith Kisor also spent hours each day helping Henry learn to speak words aloud. As Henry learned more about language, he became a skilled lip-reader.

When World War II ended, the family returned to a small town called Ho-Ho-Kus in New Jersey, where Henry's parents enrolled him in kindergarten. Henry got along well with his hearing peers, and the teachers were impressed that a boy so young could read. The principal agreed to let Henry try to stay at the school on a year-to-year basis. Thanks to his lip-reading skills, Henry did well in school. He remembers his early years as happy and ordinary.

When Henry was eight, his family moved to Evanston, Illinois, just outside of Chicago. In Evanston, the Kisors were again fortunate to encounter open-minded teachers, and Henry continued to attend regular classes with hearing children. Throughout his early years, Henry's parents encouraged him to do all the things that hearing children do. He played ball, rode a bicycle, and basically enjoyed a typical childhood. In early adolescence, however, Henry became self-conscious about his speech, which he knew sounded different from that of hearing children. Children who did not know Henry well sometimes laughed at the way he sounded. He developed a great dislike for public speaking.

Henry's self-esteem received a boost in high school, when he began to show talent as a writer. When he was a sophomore, his English teacher suggested that he enroll in a journalism course. Henry did so, and he soon discovered that he had a flair for both writing and editing. By the end of his junior year, Henry was promoted to managing editor of his high-school newspaper. Henry loved the work, and he enjoyed earning the respect of his teachers and peers.

Henry's teenage interest in journalism turned into a career. After attending Trinity College and, later, the Medill School of Journalism at Northwestern University, Henry found a job writing for the *Evening Journal*, in Wilmington, Delaware. While in Wilmington, Henry experimented in many different areas of journalism, including book reviews. Before long, Henry was writing a weekly literary column focused on local books and authors. Henry's career was developing rapidly, but he didn't like small-town life. In May 1965, he moved back to Chicago to work at a major metropolitan newspaper, the *Daily News*. Soon after returning to the Chicago area, Henry met a young woman named Debbie who was studying to become an elementary-school teacher. They began dating seriously and, on June 24, 1967, they were married.

Henry Kisor continued to prosper in his career as an editor and book reviewer. When the *Daily News* closed in 1978, he was hired immediately by another major Chicago newspaper, the *Sun-Times*. Today, Kisor continues to work for the *Sun-Times* as a literary critic and editor. In 1990, he published a book about his experiences. *What's That Pig Outdoors? A Memoir of Deafness* illustrates both the frustrations and the occasionally humorous misunderstandings that Henry Kisor encounters as a lip-reader. The title refers to an incident when one of his sons asked him, "What's that big loud noise?" To his great confusion, Henry thought the boy was asking, "What's that pig outdoors?"

As part of his responsibilities as a literary critic, Kisor must often interview authors. Lip-reading interviews can be very difficult, but he believes that he sometimes connects better with writers because of the extra effort he must put forth. He finds that technological advances and increased awareness among hearing people have made his deafness less of an obstacle to communication than it was in previous years. The Telecommunications Device for the Deaf now enables him to use the telephone to communicate with both deaf and hearing people. Computers also have opened up a new world of social interaction for Kisor and for countless other deaf or hearing-impaired people. With a computer, deaf people can communicate clearly and easily with people across the country and around the world. Closed-captioned programming has enabled Kisor to enjoy television shows with his friends and family. He also credits the Americans with Disabilities Act with creating more employment opportunities for deaf and hearing-impaired people. He believes that through increased contact, hearing people and deaf people are gaining greater understanding of one another.

"It may not often happen," says Kisor, "but when two dissimilar people—one deaf, one perhaps hearing—manage to share their humanity with one another, it can be a beautiful thing."

WILMA RUDOLPH

1940–1994

Olympic Athlete

Wilma Rudolph grew up in Clarksville, Tennessee, the sixth of eight children. Her father was a retired railroad porter, and her mother worked as a domestic. At the age of four, Wilma underwent a grueling series of illnesses—first pneumonia, then scarlet fever, and finally polio. When she regained her health at last, her left leg was paralyzed, and she was unable to walk.

Doctors in Nashville, 35 miles (56 km) away, told Mrs. Rudolph that massage and physical therapy might strengthen Wilma's legs. Determined to do everything possible for her daughter, Mrs. Rudolph learned the necessary massage techniques. Every day when she came home from work, she massaged Wilma's legs and helped her do physical therapy exercises. Wilma's brothers and sisters also learned how to give the massages and helped as much as they could. Later, Wilma's mother recalled that Wilma was rarely upset because she couldn't walk. "She tried to play. The other children came and played with her while she sat in her chair."

Gradually, Wilma's legs grew stronger. When she was eight, she learned to walk, wearing a brace and a special shoe. By the time she was eleven, she could wear regular shoes and no longer needed the brace. Almost as soon as she could walk, she developed a keen interest in athletics. She practiced shooting baskets, using a hoop her brothers put up in the backyard. By the time she was fourteen, she was an outstanding basketball player. In her sophomore year of high school, she broke a state girls' basketball record. Her basketball coach nicknamed her "Skeeter," short for mosquito, "because she was always buzzing around."

At a girls' basketball tournament in Nashville, Wilma met Ed Temple, the women's track coach at Tennessee State University. Temple was impressed by Wilma's grace and speed on the court. He was convinced that with proper training, she could become a star runner. With Temple's encouragement, Wilma went out for track and won every race she entered. "I was very competitive from the very first moment I learned that girls were allowed to run track," she said later. "From that moment, that was my world. I trained daily. . . . I would be the only girl in the stadium."

In 1957, Wilma Rudolph enrolled at Tennessee State University, a school in Nashville for African-American students. Though she trained hard, a series of illnesses and injuries kept her from competing regularly. Nevertheless, she managed to qualify for the United States Olympic Team. In 1960, she set off for the Olympic Summer Games in Rome, Italy.

Wilma Rudolph's performance at the Olympics astonished the world. She easily won the women's 100-meter dash, tying the world record of 11.3 seconds. She won the 200-meter dash, setting an Olympics record time of 23.2 seconds. Finally, she ran the last leg of the 400-meter women's relay, helping her team set a world record of 44.4 seconds.

The crowd in Italy loved the tall, slim African-American woman with the gracious smile. After the Olympics, Rudolph toured Europe, entering a series of invitational meets. In Cologne, Germany, mounted police had to hold back the throngs of people who pressed around her. In Berlin, people pounded on the windows of her bus, demanding her autograph. When she stepped out, people swarmed around her and stole her shoes.

Wilma Rudolph shows off her three 1960 Olympic medals.

Back in the United States, Wilma Rudolph remained a celebrity. Fans sent a deluge of letters and telegrams. Banquets were held in her honor. She was interviewed and photographed wherever she went. She found fame exhausting, but she carried herself with poise and dignity.

In February 1961, Wilma Rudolph entered the Millrose Games, an indoor track meet held at New York's Madison Square Garden. Usually the Millrose Games were restricted to males, so Rudolph was among the first women who had been invited to participate in thirty years. Once again, her performance was flawless. She won the 60-yard dash in 6.9 seconds, tying her own previous world record. Soon afterward, at a competition in Louisville, Kentucky, she ran the 70-yard dash in 7.8 seconds, breaking a world record of 8.2 seconds that had gone unchallenged since 1935. In July, she returned to West Germany, where she set a new women's world record of 11.2 seconds in the 100-meter dash.

Wilma Rudolph received the 1961 Sullivan Award, an honor reserved for America's most outstanding amateur athlete of the year.

Rudolph retired from competition in 1962. She felt that she had given her best to athletics, and she wanted to be remembered as she had been at the peak of her career. In the years that followed, she lived a quiet life, far from the public eye. She taught school, coached high-school basketball, and ran a community center. She married twice and had four children. Deeply committed to helping children of racial minorities, she established the Wilma Rudolph Foundation. The foundation brings women and men of achievement in many fields to speak at schools across the country.

All her life, Wilma Rudolph remembered the thrill of her racing career and the excitement of the Olympic Stadium in Rome when the crowd chanted her name. "When I was running, I had a sense of freedom, of running in the wind," she explained. "I never forgot all the years when I was a little girl and not able to be involved. When I ran, I felt like a butterfly. That feeling was always there."

THE CHALLENGE OF SPORTS

When the doctors examined Andy Leonard, a Vietnamese refugee, they shook their heads. Andy was hopelessly retarded, his adoptive parents were told. They had taken on a child who never would amount to anything. But twenty years later, in 1995, Andy Leonard was competing for a place on the U.S. Olympic weight-lifting team. The boy with no future had become a world-class athlete.

Andy Leonard is one of a million people with mental retardation who receive athletic training each year through an international organization called Special Olympics. Established in the 1960s, Special Olympics reflected two of President John F. Kennedy's leading concerns: improving conditions for people with retardation, and making Americans more physically fit. Eunice Kennedy Shriver, the president's sister, headed a commission on mental retardation, which reported in 1962 that little was being done for people with mental retardation in the United States. Young people with retardation had few opportunities to learn, to make friends, or to exercise.

During the summer of 1963, Eunice Shriver started an experimental day camp on her Maryland estate. One hundred children with mental retardation were paired with college students. The students worked with them every day on a variety of sports and other physical activities. The children swung from monkey bars, turned somersaults, and bounced on trampolines. By the end of the summer, most were stronger and more alert. They felt better about themselves, and they had fun.

Eunice Shriver's day camp served as a model for similar projects throughout the United States and Canada. Dozens of park districts and recreation centers launched sports programs for children and adults with mental retardation.

*Weight lifter
Andy Leonard*

In 1968, one thousand athletes, trained through these assorted programs, met in Chicago to compete in the first International Special Olympics Games.

At that first competition, the only events were swimming and track and field. By the 1970s, Special Olympics followed the pattern of summer and winter games that is used by the regular Olympic Games. The 1995 Special Olympics World Summer Games included teams from 146 nations.

With the help of some six hundred thousand volunteers, Special Olympics sponsors fifteen thousand local, state, and regional competitions throughout the year. Athletes are grouped according to gender, age, and athletic skill. Some people with profound retardation may lie on a mat and roll a ball a few inches; they compete with others who are at the same level. The athletes who go on to the world competition are among the best at their sport within a particular division. Winners earn gold, silver, and bronze medals, but everyone who takes part in the games is awarded a ribbon.

There are several athletic organizations of and for people with physical disabilities. Wheelchair Sports USA trains young people and adults who use wheelchairs to participate in track and field, basketball, soccer, and many other

A gymnast at the 1995 Special Olympics World Games

events. The United States Association of Blind Athletes (USABA) works with athletes who are blind or visually impaired. People with cerebral palsy compete in events sponsored by the United States Cerebral Palsy Athletic Association (USCPAA), and people of short stature can become involved in the Dwarf Athletic Association of America.

Within each of these associations, athletes are divided into categories based on their degree of disability. The USCPAA, for example, has four divisions. People in Class 1 have very limited use of their arms and legs. They compete in events that include bocci, bowling, cycling, and horseback riding. People in Class 4, who are able to walk and use their hands, take part in a variety of standard track-and-field events. Each of these four classes is subdivided into men's and women's events. USABA groups its athletes according to the amount of vision they have. Athletes in class B-3 have 20/200 vision—that is, they can see at 20 feet (6 m) what a normally sighted person sees at 200 (61 m). People in class B-1 are totally blind.

Like Special Olympics, each of these organizations works to train athletes through park districts, schools, and other local programs. Each also sponsors local, state, and regional competitions. In addition, there are international championships, such as the Pan-American Cerebral Palsy Games and the World Blind Skiing Competition.

Besides organizing competitions among people with disabilities, some of these organizations work to integrate disabled athletes into regular sports programs. USABA encourages regular high-school coaches to work with students who are blind. Most coaches fear that a blind athlete will require costly special equipment in order to take part in a sport. USABA volunteers show them that adaptations can be simple and inexpensive. For instance, a blind athlete can run on a track with the help of a sighted guide. The guide runs next to the blind person, giving him or her directions. A similar guide system is used by blind cross-country and downhill skiers.

Like Andy Leonard, many people who get their start through special athletic organizations go on to compete with nondisabled athletes. Some have achieved elite status. In 1980, a USABA swimmer named Trischa Zorn came within 1/100 of a point of qualifying for the regular U.S. Olympic team. A USCPAA member from Minnesota became a national archery champion.

A blind cyclist prepares her guide dog for a bicycle trip.

Because he had the use of only one arm, he pulled the bowstring with his teeth.

Elite competitions for athletes with physical disabilities have been held since 1948, when a British doctor named Sir Ludwig Guttman organized the first International Wheelchair Games. As the years passed, people with other disabilities had the opportunity to take part, as well. The first official Paralympic Games were held in Rome in 1960, immediately after the Olympic Games. Today the Paralympics is the pinnacle of athletic events for people with disabilities.

The Paralympic Games hold events for amputees, for people with cerebral palsy, for people who are blind or dwarfs, and for wheelchair users. Each of these categories is divided into classes based on the degree of an athlete's disability. Thus the Paralympics has more than 500 men's and women's events, compared with about 300 for the Olympics. In 1996, the Paralympics brought 3,500 athletes from 120 countries to Atlanta, Georgia. For the first time, the games had extensive television coverage and were sponsored by major corporations. In the past, the Paralympics struggled for media coverage. At last, the public is beginning to respond.

Whether or not they have a disability, all athletes compete for the same reasons. They are people who love to meet challenges, to push themselves to the limits. But many disabled athletes have still another motive. Through their achievements, they strive to show the world that disability is no obstacle to excellence. They are working to open doors for future generations of people with disabilities.

STEPHEN HAWKING

❧

1942−

Physicist

Stephen Hawking was only eight years old when he decided he was going to be a scientist. Today, he is one of the world's greatest physicists, and he is often compared to Albert Einstein. Like Einstein, Stephen Hawking explores the mysteries of the universe. Hawking is known throughout the world for his startling theories about so-called black holes in space. At present, Stephen Hawking is trying to succeed where even Einstein failed. He is searching for a single mathematical equation that will describe the entire universe and the forces that govern it.

Stephen William Hawking was born on January 8, 1942, in Oxford, England. The oldest of four children, Hawking was raised in a very close, scholarly family. Stephen spent most of his youth in London and in nearby St. Albans. At age eleven, Stephen Hawking entered St. Albans School, where he prepared to attend Oxford University. Stephen's father, a doctor and research biologist, hoped his oldest son would one day study medicine at Oxford. But young Stephen had his own ideas. By the time he was fourteen years old, he had chosen physics as his special area of interest. Physics is the study of matter, energy, and the laws that govern their behavior. Through physics, Stephen

Hawking hoped to answer his many questions about the universe.

Though he was obviously smart, Stephen did not distinguish himself at St. Albans. In fact, his parents feared he would not gain admittance to Oxford. They need not have worried, however. Stephen did very well on the entrance examinations and entered Oxford in 1959.

At Oxford, Stephen was popular with the other students, but he did not apply himself to his studies. He listened to classical music, read science fiction, and enjoyed himself. He was also for a time the coxswain (or leader) of one of the Oxford rowing teams. Though he remained interested in physics and mathematics, the courses at Oxford were not difficult enough to challenge him, and he was rather bored.

Hawking began his graduate studies at Cambridge University in 1962. At about this time, he noticed that he stumbled frequently. When he spoke, his words were often slurred. Small tasks, such as tying his shoes, became difficult. In January 1963, when Hawking was barely twenty-one years old, doctors diagnosed his disease as amyotrophic lateral sclerosis (ALS). Also called Lou Gehrig's disease (after the famous baseball player who died of ALS in 1941), ALS attacks the nerves that govern voluntary movements—those activities that we can control, such as walking and speaking. ALS does not affect involuntary movements, such as the beating of the heart, but it can eventually hinder breathing and swallowing. Doctors told Stephen Hawking he probably would die within two years.

At first, Hawking was depressed. He saw no point in continuing his studies. Before long, though, his optimism returned. The disease seemed to be progressing more slowly than expected. He began to realize he needed a healthy mind to be a scientist, but not necessarily a healthy body. He approached his work with renewed interest and completed his Ph.D. in 1966. Then he became a member of the Cambridge faculty. His work as a teacher was excellent, and Hawking received many promotions. In 1977, Cambridge honored Stephen Hawking by creating a special position for him. At age thirty-five, he became

Students listen intently to Stephen Hawking during a lecture at Northeastern University in Boston.

the first Professor of Gravitational Physics at Cambridge. Two years later, Hawking achieved the highest position available at Cambridge when he became a Lucasian Professor of Mathematics.

Stephen Hawking's calculations are so complex that many scientists cannot fully understand them. But his basic ideas are fascinating, even to readers who are not trained physicists. In 1988, Stephen Hawking published a book for the public called *A Brief History of Time: From the Big Bang to Black Holes* in which he tried to explain his ideas simply, without using equations. *A Brief History of Time* quickly became a best-seller, and it even was made into a movie.

Since his early thirties, Stephen Hawking has used a wheelchair. He is capable of very little movement and has trouble holding his head up. In 1985, he lost the ability to speak. He communicates through a special computer that displays lists of words on a screen. Using the few fingers he still is able to move, Hawking squeezes a lever to select words. The computer displays his sentences on the screen for others to read. It even "speaks" for him with an electronic voice.

Despite his disease, Stephen Hawking considers himself a fortunate person. He is glad he chose to be a physicist because he can do all of his work with his mind. Thus, Hawking says, his disability "has not been a serious handicap."

I. KING JORDAN

1943–

Educator

When he was in high school, no one could have guessed that Irving King Jordan would someday become a university president. He had been a poor student all his life and took almost no interest in school. The one class he really enjoyed was typing, where he was the only boy and could flirt with girls. He was lively and popular, the life of any party. He graduated from school with a C average. In the yearbook, he was voted Class Clown.

After high school, Jordan enlisted in the U.S. Navy. He soon realized he had no taste for military routine. After his discharge, he still had no idea what he wanted to do with his life. He worked at an assortment of jobs and spent his spare time riding his motorcycle and dancing in nightclubs.

Jordan's life changed in an instant one night in 1964, when he was twenty-one years old. His motorcycle struck an oncoming car, and his skull was fractured. The paramedics who rushed to the scene thought he was dying and called for a priest. In the hospital, a neurosurgeon told Jordan's parents to pray for his death. If he survived, the doctor told them, he would be in a hopeless coma.

I. King Jordan spent the next fourteen months in the hospital. To the amazement of the doctors, his mind was entirely unimpaired. But the accident left Jordan totally deaf.

After the accident, Jordan had to adjust to a whole new way of life. He could speak, but he could not understand words that were spoken to him. Whether he was with old friends or complete strangers, the simplest communication was suddenly difficult. Yet he did not sink into despair. Instead, he began to make new plans. "You would think the accident would have narrowed my world, limited me," he explained later. "It did the exact opposite. I started to pay attention to the world instead of taking it for granted." He decided to go to college and enrolled at Gallaudet University in Washington, D.C.

Gallaudet was founded in 1864 as the nation's first, and only, institution of higher education for people who were deaf. When Jordan arrived in the fall of 1966, he found himself in the midst of a flourishing deaf community. All around him, students conversed in American Sign Language. Their flying fingers telegraphed messages that Jordan had not yet learned to read. The Gallaudet students did not feel ashamed of their deafness. They did not think they were inferior to people who could hear. United by a common language, they had a strong sense of cultural identity.

Among students who had been deaf all their lives, Jordan felt like an outsider. He found the culture interesting, but he did not feel a part of it. "For years I thought I was only a visitor to the silent world, which made me a loner in college," he said later. "I was no longer fully accepted by hearing people, and not knowing the customs of the deaf world, I was socially awkward around other deaf students." He began to learn American Sign Language and gradually felt more comfortable and more fully accepted.

In the late 1960s, deaf people encountered a wall of discrimination in American society. Graduates of Gallaudet found few opportunities for employment. Most employers believed that a deaf person was incapable of holding a responsible job. But Jordan was shocked that such prejudice lurked even on the Gallaudet campus. Though the student body was almost entirely deaf, the administration and faculty were composed largely of hearing people. Jordan and his classmates believed that the hearing officials of the university treated the deaf students as if they were children. The student health center even hired a pediatrician (a doctor who treats babies and children) to care for the students. In 1967, the students protested this policy until a regular doctor was finally hired.

Jordan studied extremely hard at Gallaudet. After graduating in 1970, he enrolled in a Ph.D. program in psychology at the University of Tennessee. He spent most of his time in the library. By reading voraciously, he absorbed the material that other students heard during lectures.

I. King Jordan obtained his doctoral degree in 1973 and returned to Gallaudet as an assistant professor of psychology. His students found him warm, charming, and endlessly available. He always was interested in their problems and dreams. Over the following years, he was granted several promotions. In 1986, he became dean of the College of Arts and Sciences.

Jordan loved his work at Gallaudet, but he was reminded every day that the university's administrators and board of directors doubted the abilities of deaf people. In a thousand subtle ways, Gallaudet reinforced the notion that people who could hear were superior to those who could not.

In December 1987, Gallaudet's president, Jerry C. Lee, announced his resignation. In its 124-year history, Gallaudet had had six presidents, all of them hearing. Students argued that it was now time for the university to choose a deaf president. In February 1988, the board of trustees announced that three candidates were being considered for the presidency. Two of them were deaf, and one was hearing. One of the two deaf candidates was Dean I. King Jordan.

On March 1, hundreds of students gathered for a mass rally, demanding that the board select one of the deaf candidates. On March 6, the board announced the final decision. Gallaudet's seventh president would be the hearing candidate, Elizabeth Zinser.

The following day, outraged students and their supporters shut down the campus. They blocked its entrances with parked cars and buses and boycotted all classes. They gathered in a mass demonstration, shouting and signing slogans. Protestors marched on the administration building, wearing placards that proclaimed DEAF POWER! and FIGHT FOR DEAF PRESIDENT! At last, Jane Bassett Spillman, a member of the board of trustees, appeared to address the crowd. She did not know sign language, and spoke through an interpreter. "The selection process was lawful, proper, and final," she stated. Some people in the crowd claim that she added, "Deaf people are not yet ready to function in the hearing world." Spillman later denied making this comment, but it was repeated continuously throughout the deaf community, fanning the flames of anger.

On March 8, students organized a massive protest on Washington's Pennsylvania Avenue. They marched toward the White House, backing up traffic for miles. The Deaf President Now movement won words of support from some of the nation's most prominent political leaders, including Jesse Jackson, Senator Robert Dole, and President George Bush.

Throughout these days of upheaval, I. King Jordan was in torment. His heart was with the deaf students, so long denied a sense of worth and dignity. Yet, as a college dean, he felt that he must uphold the board's decision. On March 9, at Spillman's request, he made a public statement in support of Elizabeth Zinser.

That evening, the Gallaudet faculty cast an overwhelming vote demanding the board rescind its decision. The following day, Jordan called a press conference and declared, "Yesterday . . . I gave a statement recognizing the legal authority of the board to name the president of Gallaudet. In fact, my personal reaction to the board's decision was and is anger at the continuing lack of confidence they have shown in deaf people. I must now publicly affirm my support for the point of view held by the Gallaudet community." Jordan finally had taken his stand with the deaf community, as one of its proud members.

In the stormy days that followed, both Jane Spillman and President-Elect

Elizabeth Zinser resigned. On March 13, the board of trustees appointed I. King Jordan to serve as president of Gallaudet University.

The Gallaudet Uprising, as it came to be called, received nationwide coverage in the press. It raised the awareness of millions of people who never before had thought about the rights and abilities of deaf citizens. On October 23, newspapers across the country printed the stirring words of Jordan's inaugural address: "This is an event made possible because so many of you watching today were willing to commit yourselves to a cause that you believed just and right—the right of every person to have unlimited goals and expectations. . . . Last March, in our unity, in our belief, and in our amazement at our own strength, we enjoyed a true renaissance, a motivation found. I challenge you to take up this motivation, take up this enthusiasm, take up this new courage, and to try and do anything under the sun. I challenge you to succeed."

Jordan's high profile in the press gave him a chance to become a national spokesman for deaf people. Despite his heavy responsibilities as university president, he finds time to travel the country, speaking to business and civic groups. He is especially concerned with expanding the employment options for people who are deaf.

After Jordan became president, many Gallaudet students expected the university to be transformed overnight. They wanted the administration to present a revolutionary outlook toward deafness. But many old-timers remained on the board of trustees, balking at every innovation. "Revolutionaries want to see changes right away," Jordan reflects. "Don't try to make me make changes in one month, two months, or six. Look back five years from now. Then you'll be able to see results."

JUDI CHAMBERLIN

1944–

Mental Patients'
Liberation Activist

"I had a pretty normal childhood—if growing up in Brooklyn is ever normal," states Judi Chamberlin. She was a quiet, serious girl who loved to read. But she didn't enjoy school and had no interest in attending college. After high school, she worked as a secretary and married at the age of twenty.

Judi and her husband loved to talk about the big house and wonderful children they would have someday. In the meantime, they rented a tiny apartment and struggled to keep ahead of the bills. Judi was thrilled when she discovered that she was pregnant. Then, three months later, she had a miscarriage. The loss of her unborn baby left her inconsolable. People urged her to get over it, to get back to her normal routine. But she only wanted to be alone with her terrible sadness.

Distressed by her crying and withdrawal, Judi's family took her to a psychiatrist. He prescribed an assortment of tranquilizers, but Judi only slipped deeper into despair. Finally the psychiatrist suggested that she should be admitted to a mental hospital. Judi went willingly, convinced that at last she would receive the help she needed.

Judi Chamberlin spent the next six months in and out of psychiatric hospitals. The nurses and doctors did not encourage her to talk about her problems. Instead they treated her almost exclusively with medication. The drugs made her lethargic and confused. Rather than feeling better, she felt increasingly certain that there was something terribly wrong with her.

As a psychiatric patient, Judi discovered that she had no legal rights. Her clothes and other belongings were taken from her—supposedly for safekeeping. Every minute of her day was strictly regimented. She could not make phone calls or receive visitors without permission from the staff. The doors were locked, and only the staff had the keys.

When Judi failed to improve in a private hospital, she was told that she could stay there no longer. She would have to be transferred to Rockland State Hospital in Orangeburg, New York. Judi was horrified. This was the end of the line, the final proof that her case was hopeless. She received permission to make a few phone calls and contacted the Legal Aid Society and the American Civil Liberties Union (ACLU). These organizations were supposed to protect the rights of citizens. But no one wanted to hear her story. "If that's where the doctors want to send you," she was told, "then that's where you need to be."

Rockland State Hospital was even worse than she had imagined. All day long a television and a radio blared simultaneously. The food was so dreadful that she could eat little besides bread and margarine. There was no privacy. In the bathroom, there were not even stalls around the toilets. Nurses and attendants herded the patients from place to place with no explanation or apology, as though they were not really people. Yet in this prisonlike atmosphere, Judi found a few real friends among her fellow patients. They listened to each other and offered whatever comfort they could.

One day an aide brought in a set of plastic bowling pins. To the delight of the patients, she organized a series of relay races on the ward. The races were a shocking and happy break from the dreary hospital routine. But Judi realized that the game was silly and childish. She felt disgusted with herself for enjoying it so much.

Judy knew that if she was ever going to get out of Rockland State, she would have to convince the staff that she was getting well. She was more miserable than ever, but she learned to hide her true feelings. She dressed neatly and helped keep the ward clean. She cried only at night, in bed, muffling her sobs in her pillow.

Eventually Judi convinced the doctors that she was cured. After sixty days, she was discharged from the hospital. Once she was free, she decided that she must stay away from the mental-health system at any cost. In the years that followed, Judi Chamberlin kept her psychiatric history a secret. She and her husband had a daughter, Julie, but the marriage ended in divorce. Judi moved from city to city, seeking direction for her life.

By 1971, Judi Chamberlin was back in New York. One day she saw a notice in the paper about the Mental Patients' Liberation Project. The notice described a group of former psychiatric patients who got together for mutual support. The former patients also worked on ways to change the mental-health system. When she attended her first meeting, Judi felt that she had come home at last. Like her, the people who sat in the meeting room were survivors of a system that had made them feel dehumanized. They felt that they had been treated as criminals simply for being unhappy, and that they had been punished cruelly.

The Mental Patients' Liberation Project (MPLP) questioned the very existence of "mental illness." Were there really diseases of the mind that could be "treated" and "cured" like physical ailments? Or were mental hospitals filled with people who had crumbled under intolerable stress? Clearly the brutal conditions in some hospitals did not help people; the hospitals only made it harder for people to rebuild their lives. Somehow there had to be a better approach, a way to help people cope with their problems and move ahead.

As a member of the MPLP, Judi Chamberlin wrote articles and appeared on radio talk shows. At first, she concealed her identity by using a false name, but finally she decided to use her real name. The MPLP members helped each other realize that they had no reason to be ashamed. They had done nothing wrong; they had nothing to hide. Only by coming forward, strong and unafraid, could they hope to bring about change.

In 1974, Judi Chamberlin moved to Vancouver, British Columbia, with a man she had fallen in love with. Soon after they were settled in their new home, the relationship collapsed. Again Judi found herself overwhelmed with sadness. Her life seemed empty, utterly without meaning.

Instead of going to a psychiatrist, Judi turned to an innovative program called the Vancouver Emotional Emergency Center. When she arrived at the center, she was greeted by two staff members, who listened sympathetically to her story. Judi sensed their warmth and their sincere caring. When she explained that she was afraid to be alone, they said she could sleep on a couch in the center's living room. For the next several days she remained at the center. When she cried, no one told her to stop. When she needed to talk, someone was always there to listen. Slowly she felt her strength returning, and at last she was ready to be on her own once more.

Judi moved to Boston and cofounded a group of psychiatric survivors called the Mental Patients Liberation Front (MPLF). Her experience in Vancouver helped her to envision many new ways in which people could be helped in times of crisis. With others in the MPLF, she worked to create a program staffed entirely by former patients. In traditional hospitals, there always was a vast difference between the "sick" patients and the "healthy" staff. The staff had almost limitless power over the patients' lives. Such inequality did not exist in the self-help centers set up by MPLF and similar groups. Pain was acknowledged as one unavoidable aspect of being human. As travelers on the same journey, people helped one another through difficult times.

In 1978, Judi Chamberlin published a book, *On Our Own: Patient-Controlled Alternatives to the Mental Health System.* She made numerous public appearances and was a guest on the television talk show *Good Morning America.* In her talks and articles, she pleaded for an end to involuntary commitment and the inappropriate use of drugs to treat psychiatric patients. She urged a complete overhaul of the mental-health system. She called for the establishment of a nationwide network of self-help programs run by, and for, the "mentally ill."

Not surprisingly, most psychiatrists and other mental-health professionals objected to Judi Chamberlin's ideas. Mental illness rendered people incapable of making sound decisions, they insisted. Mental patients could not manage their own lives, so certainly they were in no position to help others. Yet Judi remembered the friends she had made at Rockland State. From her own experience, she knew that people in trouble had a wonderful ability to help each other.

Year by year, the self-help movement gained momentum. Self-help centers opened all over the country. More professionals began to take the movement seriously. Judi Chamberlin's book was translated into Italian and Japanese as her ideas spread abroad. In the United States, she has led the fight to protect the rights of patients in psychiatric hospitals.

In 1985, Judi Chamberlin helped to found the Ruby Rogers Advocacy and Drop-In Center in Somerville, Massachusetts. Open seven days a week, the center is a resource in such areas as housing, education, employment, and recreation. And someone is always there when a visitor just wants to talk. Judi Chamberlin is also the founder of the National Empowerment Center in Lawrence, Massachusetts, an organization that provides information about alternative programs for psychiatric survivors. At Boston University's Center for Psychiatric Rehabilitation, she conducts research on self-help and other nontraditional approaches to emotional problems.

Judi Chamberlin is recognized as an international leader in the mental patients' self-help movement. She received the Distinguished Service Award of the President of the United States from the President's Committee on Employment of People with Disabilities in 1992, and the N. Neal Pike Prize for Service to People with Disabilities from Boston University Law School in 1995.

WILMA MANKILLER

∽

1945–

Principal Chief of the Cherokee Nation

When she was a small child, Wilma Mankiller's father told her that the family's surname had been given to one of their warrior ancestors as a high military honor. It was part of her Cherokee heritage, a heritage in which he urged her to take pride.

But it was not always easy to feel proud growing up in the poverty-stricken Cherokee country of northeastern Oklahoma. Wilma Mankiller was one of eleven children. Her family struggled to survive on a 160-acre (65-hectare) farm called Mankiller Flats. The farmhouse had no plumbing or electricity. The land had been given to Wilma's grandfather in the 1800s by the U.S. government after the Cherokees were forcibly moved to Oklahoma from their homeland in North Carolina.

When Wilma was twelve, the family farm failed. The Bureau of Indian Affairs (BIA), a branch of the U.S. Department of the Interior, relocated the Mankillers to San Francisco, California. At that time, the BIA encouraged Native Americans to leave reservations and move into mainstream America, where jobs were more available. Wilma found the adjustment to city life painful and difficult. Later she remembered, "One day I was out here, and the next day

I was trying to deal with the mysteries of television, indoor plumbing, neon lights, and elevators." Impoverished as the farm had been, the Mankillers had known a sense of community as part of the Cherokee tribe. In San Francisco, that community spirit was missing.

During the 1960s, Wilma Mankiller took college courses and became a social worker. She married an accountant from Ecuador, had two daughters, and tried to live as a homemaker in the San Francisco suburbs. But she was restless and discontented. She needed something more, but she didn't know what it was. In 1969, a group of Native American college students occupied the former federal prison on Alcatraz Island in San Francisco Bay. Their action was a protest against the government's treatment of Native American people. The spirit of the rising Indian rights movement captured Wilma's imagination. As the mother of young children, she could not join the protesters on the island. But she threw herself into fund-raising, and for the next eighteen months, she worked tirelessly to support the demonstrators.

The Alcatraz protest changed Wilma Mankiller's life. She went back to college and took a job coordinating Native American programs with the Oakland, California, school system. After ten years of marriage, she divorced her husband and returned to Mankiller Flats, where she built a small frame house for herself and the girls. She wanted her daughters to experience real life and to know their Cherokee heritage. She hoped that her firsthand knowledge of mainstream America could be of use to the Cherokee people.

In 1977, Wilma Mankiller took the position of Economic Stimulus Coordinator for the Cherokee Nation. In 1981, she established and became director of the Cherokee Nation's Community Development Department, raising the necessary funds herself. She firmly believed that Indians must and could solve their own economic problems. She helped the Cherokee build better houses and lay down new water lines to isolated rural areas.

Wilma Mankiller found her work with the Cherokee Nation intensely rewarding. At the same time, she fulfilled another dream, completing her B.A.

at Flaming Rainbows University in Stillwell, Oklahoma. She also took graduate courses in community planning at the University of Arkansas.

Just when she seemed to be building the life she had always wanted, Wilma Mankiller was confronted with an ordeal she had never imagined. In 1979, she was in a head-on automobile collision on an Oklahoma highway. One of her closest friends was killed in the accident, and Mankiller was so severely injured that she required seventeen operations.

While Mankiller was in the hospital, doctors became concerned about a strange muscular weakness that seemed unrelated to her injuries. A series of tests revealed that she had a rare form of muscular dystrophy. Muscular dystrophy is a disease that causes the body's muscles to deteriorate, making it increasingly difficult for the person to speak and move. In Mankiller's case, treatment with medication slowed the progress of the disease. Looking back at that period in her life, Wilma Mankiller says, "Everything has been up from that point on. In a way, it seems it was a test of perseverance. It was a maturing kind of process. It was a definite preparation."

In 1983, Ross O. Swimmer ran for the office of principal chief of the Cherokee Nation and selected Wilma Mankiller as his running mate. He was a Republican, and she was a liberal Democrat, but Swimmer held a deep respect for her and for her work. "She knows her strengths and her weaknesses," he explained, "and she is one sharp businesswoman." When Swimmer was elected, Wilma Mankiller became the Cherokee Nation's first woman deputy chief.

Halfway through his four-year term, Swimmer was appointed Assistant Secretary of the Interior for Indian Affairs, and left Oklahoma for Washington, D.C. On December 15, 1985, Wilma Mankiller was sworn in as principal chief of the Cherokee Nation. She was the first woman ever to hold such a high-ranking position in a major North American tribal government. With more than ninety thousand members, the Cherokee Nation was small in numbers, but it had settled the fourteen counties of northeastern Oklahoma, as well as parts of four other states. Its annual budget amounted to forty-eight million dollars. As chief, Wilma Mankiller had more power than most members of the U.S. Congress. Mankiller proved to be an excellent leader, and in 1987 and 1991, she won reelection.

As tribal chief, Mankiller worked to develop job opportunities in the community, chiseling away at the Cherokees' 50 percent unemployment rate. She launched the Institute for Cherokee Literacy, a summer program to teach reading and writing in the Cherokee language. Always she stressed the need for Indians to work together, solving their own problems through community action.

As a female chief, Mankiller knew that the Cherokee Nation and the world were watching her closely. "I'm conscious of the fact that I am the first female chief . . . and I want to make sure I do a good job," she stated. "So I feel like I have to do a little extra."

ITZHAK PERLMAN

⌒

1945–

Violinist

As far back as he can remember, Itzhak Perlman wanted to play the violin. His vocation came to him at the age of three, when he heard a violin recital on the radio. He began playing a toy fiddle, trying to re-create the glorious sounds he had heard. Itzhak's parents, Polish Jews who had immigrated to Israel, were thrilled by their son's interest in music. For about six dollars, they bought him a full-sized violin in a secondhand store. Though the family's finances were limited, they arranged for him to take music lessons.

When he was four, Itzhak Perlman contracted poliomyelitis. The disease weakened the muscles in his legs, and afterward he used leg braces and crutches to help him walk. A year passed before he recovered completely, but he managed to practice the violin every day.

With a scholarship from the America-Israel Cultural Foundation, Itzhak Perlman entered the Tel Aviv Academy of Music when he was five years old. He soon was hailed as a musical prodigy, performing frequently with symphonies in Tel Aviv and Jerusalem. He gave his first solo recital when he was ten.

News of the gifted young violinist reached the United States. Ed Sullivan, host of a popular television variety show, arranged for Itzhak Perlman to be a guest on his program. Perlman dazzled a nationwide audience with his performance of Rimsky-Korsakov's "The Flight of the Bumblebee" and excerpts from Mendelssohn's violin concerto. He decided to continue his studies in the United States, and his parents left Israel to be with him.

Itzhak Perlman enrolled in a special high-school program at the renowned Juilliard School for the Performing Arts in New York City. His routine of classes and practice sessions often was interrupted by performance tours with the New York Youth Symphony and the National Orchestral Foundation. Perlman made his debut at Carnegie Hall on March 5, 1963. His performance brought him to the attention of Isaac Stern and Yehudi Menuhin, two of the world's leading violinists.

In April 1964, Itzhak Perlman became a finalist in the Edward M. Levintripp International Competition. With the three other top contestants, he performed works by Bach, Mozart, and Tchaikovsky before a panel of judges at Carnegie Hall. The youngest of the finalists, Perlman was awarded the highly prestigious Levintripp Prize. The *New York Herald Tribune* praised his playing for its "warmth and individuality, its big rich tone and faultless intonation." In addition to the thousand-dollar prize, Perlman won the opportunity to make solo appearances with the New York Philharmonic, the Cleveland Orchestra,

*Itzhak Perlman
in concert*

and several other major symphony orchestras across the country.

Wherever he went, Perlman won the hearts of his listeners. Returning to Israel on a concert tour, he received a fifteen-minute standing ovation in Tel Aviv. When he gave his first performance with the New York Philharmonic, he got five curtain calls. Perlman played at Carnegie Hall in a memorial concert for the U.S. senator and statesman Adlai Stevenson in October 1965. A music critic for the *New Yorker* glowed, "There is nothing in the whole field of violin playing that he cannot do. I cannot remember when a first encounter with a violinist has made such an impression on me."

Because of his difficulty with walking and standing, Perlman plays the violin while sitting in a chair. During his early years as a concert performer, he would take his place on stage before the audience entered the auditorium. Perlman did this to avoid drawing attention to his disability. In the late 1970s, he became aware of the growing disability rights movement. He developed a sense of solidarity with other disabled people, and he realized that for years he had felt ashamed of his disability. When he realized it was not something he must hide, Perlman began walking out on stage using his crutches in full view of the audience.

Itzhak Perlman is married to violinist Tobi Lynn Friedlander; the couple has five children. He keeps up with a heavy concert schedule, teaches violin, and does fund-raising for organizations of people with disabilities. After four decades as a performer, Perlman still loves to play for an audience. "Nothing bothers me," he once told the *New York Times*. "I'm never afraid of an audience. You have to be a little bit of a ham to enjoy the audience, and I do."

1946–

Actor

W hen thirteen-year-old Patty Duke starred as Helen Keller in William Gibson's play *The Miracle Worker*, the *New York Times* raved: "Little Miss Duke is altogether superb. . . . Although her performance is necessarily wordless, it is completely articulate." Patty had spent weeks in preparation before she auditioned for the part of the young Helen Keller. Through most of the play, she had to portray a child who was blind, deaf, and had no concept of language. Patty practiced eating, dressing, and moving about while wearing a blindfold. She trained herself not to react to bright lights or to sudden, loud noises. She learned the manual alphabet, the set of hand shapes that represent letters for people who are deaf. When she finally auditioned after all this training, she easily won the role of Helen Keller. The play was such a success that it was voted Best Play of 1962 by drama critics, and Patty went on to star in the motion-picture version. In 1963, she became the youngest performer to win an Academy Award in a regular category—Best Supporting Actress.

Yet despite her professional success, Patty Duke was deeply unhappy. From her earliest childhood, she had experienced panic attacks—sudden bouts of overwhelming terror that sent her screaming through the house. When she was eighteen, she had a severe manic episode. She believed that voices of unseen strangers were giving her secret messages. She talked incessantly, night and day. After a few weeks, she plunged into a terrible depression. She felt so sad and worthless that she couldn't get out of bed.

Through the years that followed, Patty Duke managed to function as an actor, living and working in front of millions of people. But her personal life was a shambles as she bounced from frantic mania to the depths of despair, never able to find a healthy balance. Twice she married and divorced. With her family, she flew into violent rages, hurling dishes and smashing furniture. Frequently she attempted to take her own life. "I was completely unraveling and beyond anyone's control, least of all my own," she recalled later. "I just wanted the pain to stop. The only thoughts that went through my head were, 'Please make this stop! Please make me brave enough to die so this anguish will stop!'"

Finally, in 1982, a psychiatrist told her that he suspected she had manic-depressive disorder, a disease caused by a chemical imbalance in the brain. Patty was elated at the news. Those two linked words, mania and depression, described her existence. For the first time, the torment she had experienced throughout most of her life had a name.

The psychiatrist treated Patty Duke with a drug called lithium, which is often helpful to people with manic depression. Within three weeks, she began to feel better. "It wasn't anything dramatic," she explained in an interview. "I just felt a calmness I had never known. Things were just easier. It was easier to get up, easier to carry on a conversation with somebody. It was easier to be. For the first time in my life I felt normal."

Lithium did not solve all of Duke's problems. Manic-depressive disease did not go away, but its symptoms were easier to control. Stress or lack of sleep still could pitch her into a frenzy. But gradually she learned how to avoid most flare-ups.

In 1986, Patty Duke married Mike Pierce and began to build a new life. She continued to appear in made-for-television movies and won three Emmy awards. But she was painfully aware that millions of others, less fortunate than herself, struggled from day to day with manic-depressive disease and other mental illnesses. Public fear and misunderstanding were enormous. Many people were so ashamed that they tried to hide their pain and terror from the world.

Patty Duke decided to go public with her personal story. Perhaps, she reasoned, her status as a celebrity could free others from the sense of stigma they endured. She wanted to show that mental illnesses are diseases, just like diabetes or cancer. Most of all, she wanted to offer hope that people with mental illness can recover and live rewarding lives.

During the late 1980s and 1990s, Patty Duke toured the country. She talked to psychiatric patients and their families, to doctors and social workers, to church groups and Rotary Clubs. She testified before congressional committees and spoke on behalf of the National Institute of Mental Health. She touched thousands of lives with her openness on a subject once considered unspeakable.

HARILYN ROUSSO

1946–

Disability Rights Activist, Psychotherapist

When Harilyn Rousso began piano lessons as a child, she was frustrated by many of the pieces she had to learn. The part for the right hand was always the most complex, yet it was her left hand that had the best coordination. After much practice, she found a perfect solution to the problem. She simply crossed her hands and played the difficult right-hand part with her more agile left hand, and used her right hand for the easier, left-hand part. It was unconventional, but it worked.

Harilyn Rousso had cerebral palsy, a condition that is usually caused at birth by a lack of oxygen to the brain. Cerebral palsy can take many forms. In Harilyn's case, it affected her speech and coordination. She could perform most tasks, although sometimes (such as when she played the piano) she had to find her own methods. Though she had few actual limitations, most people thought of her as "disabled." They focused on her limping walk, her shaky hands, and her unsteady speech. She felt she was branded as "different."

Harilyn attended regular public school in Queens, New York, at a time when most children with disabilities were placed in segregated classes. If any of her teachers threatened Harilyn with special treatment, her mother marched into school and laid down the law. Harilyn was a normal child, her parents insisted. She was to be treated like everybody else.

In elementary school, Harilyn made friends easily and felt accepted as one of the girls. But when she reached junior high, everything changed. Her girlfriends turned boy-crazy overnight. They fussed endlessly over their appearance and talked of nothing but dating and going steady. Harilyn was as boy-crazy as all the other girls, but she found that boys ignored her—except for one, who made his friends laugh by imitating the way she walked. Everyone seemed to believe that having a perfect body was the only important human quality. No one said so directly, but Harilyn sensed that she had been disqualified from the social lives of all her friends.

Harilyn had no contact with other disabled teenagers or adults. At home, no one ever talked about her cerebral palsy or the prejudice she encountered. Her parents had worked very hard to help her be "normal," and they found it hard to discuss painful issues related to her disability.

During high school, Harilyn studied constantly and earned top grades. She did well in math and decided to major in economics when she went to college. She enrolled at Brandeis University in Waltham, Massachusetts, living away from home for the first time. During her freshman year, she was achingly homesick. In a tearful telephone conversation one night, she told her father that she couldn't make it and wanted to leave school. To her amazement, he didn't argue with her. "All right," he said. "Come home, if that's what you want to do." Suddenly she realized that she wasn't ready to quit yet. She determined to stay at college and make the best of the experience. As time passed, she found friends and began to enjoy college life.

After graduating from Brandeis, Harilyn worked as an assistant to an economist. When she went for her job interview, she discovered that the economist was a woman with cerebral palsy. Harilyn had met very few people with disabilities before, and never a disabled woman who was so bright, attractive, and successful. To her delight, Harilyn learned that the economist was married.

Harilyn had never known a disabled woman who was in a romantic relationship. She didn't believe that such a thing was possible.

Later Harilyn worked with the Office of Economic Opportunity (OEO) in Washington, D.C. While she lived in Washington, she became involved in the growing women's movement. In a weekly "consciousness-raising" group, she and several other women exchanged thoughts and feelings about issues in their lives. Harilyn was the only woman in the group who had a disability. Yet, to her surprise, she found that the others shared many of her concerns about relationships and physical appearance. She was not alone after all.

The consciousness-raising group showed Harilyn that she had the ability to listen to people and draw them out. She decided to explore careers that would involve interpersonal relations. She attended graduate school and earned her degree in social work. For several years, she worked as a social worker, counseling people with a variety of troubles. She then decided she wanted to become a psychotherapist and enrolled in a training program. From the beginning, the training staff questioned whether someone with a disability could work effectively with patients. Eventually Harilyn was dropped from the program.

Harilyn was devastated. She had always been a high achiever, but now her confidence was shaken. As she thought over what had happened, she became convinced that the training institute had treated her unfairly. Somewhere there must be other people with disabilities working as psychotherapists. Harilyn resolved to track them down and learn about their experiences.

As she hoped, Harilyn found several disabled women and men who were psychotherapists in the New York area. She also met others who had been refused admission to training programs solely because they were disabled. For the first time, she fully recognized that people with disabilities were subject to prejudice and discrimination.

Harilyn Rousso's concern with women's issues and disability issues led to her special interest in the experiences of disabled women. The women's movement barely acknowledged that disabled women existed, and the disability rights movement seldom addressed the specific needs of women in the disabled community. Because some people found her speech hard to understand, Harilyn had never liked talking before groups. But now she found herself speaking about women with disabilities at mental health centers, women's conferences, and disability rights conventions. At Rutgers University, she delivered a lecture to two hundred nurses and medical students.

Harilyn Rousso was keenly aware of the gaps in her own childhood. She wanted to help teenage girls with disabilities to believe in themselves. She wished she could show them that work, marriage, and children were all within their reach. In the early 1980s, she helped design an innovative program called the Networking Project for Disabled Women and Girls. Sponsored by the YWCA of the City of New York, the project introduced disabled girls to women with disabilities from a wide range of backgrounds. Most women with disabilities were eager to take part in the program. They had grown up in isolation, unable to talk to anyone about their deepest feelings. They hoped to improve life for the next generation.

Disabled girls, however, were less willing to get involved. They were chiefly interested in fitting in with their nondisabled classmates. Few had any desire to spend time talking to a bunch of adults who used crutches, wheelchairs, or dog guides. Harilyn visited schools and church groups, camps and youth centers. She arranged transportation for girls who could not use the inaccessible subways and buses. Little by little, teens came to the Y for group discussions and parties. They met deaf women who worked as teachers and technicians, and blind women who were lawyers, secretaries, and social workers. Whatever their disabilities and occupations might be, the women talked freely about all aspects of their lives. They spoke of hurt and disappointment as well as triumph. They talked about discrimination and described their strategies for survival.

The girls had a lot to learn from the older women, but they had a great deal to teach as well. They were growing up in a very different world. The women's movement and the disability rights movement had opened many new doors. Yet at the same time, girls of the 1980s had to cope with drugs, violence, and other stresses that were almost unknown when Harilyn Rousso went to school. The Mentoring Project created a dialogue between the generations that was exciting and enriching to all who took part. During the 1980s and 1990s, similar programs sprang up in cities across the country. Harilyn Rousso's work showed parents and teachers that girls with disabilities had special concerns that should not be ignored.

In 1988, Harilyn Rousso edited a book for young people, *Disabled, Female, and Proud*. The book is based on interviews with ten women with disabilities. She also served as executive producer for a video entitled "Positive Images: Portraits of Women with Disabilities."

Harilyn Rousso left the Mentoring Project in 1990. She continues consulting with agencies that serve young people. Her goal is to see girls with disabilities fully included on every level of community life—at school, at church, at the Y, and on the organizing committee for the senior prom. She never tires of talking with disabled girls, listening to their points of view, and helping them to make their voices heard.

FOR THE DISABLED, OF THE DISABLED

⌒

The United Nations (UN) planned 1981 as a special year. It would launch a decade-long series of worldwide programs to heighten awareness about disability issues. The UN intended to call 1981 the International Year for Disabled Persons.

Many people with disabilities were dismayed by the name the UN had chosen. They felt that 1981 should not be the year *for*, but the year *of* disabled persons. Frank Bowe, a disability rights activist who is deaf, spearheaded the U.S. campaign to change the name. He explained that throughout history, people with disabilities have had few opportunities to speak for themselves. Other people—relatives, teachers, doctors, social workers—traditionally acted on behalf of disabled people, claiming to know what was best. Not until the rise of the disability rights movement in the early 1970s did large numbers of people with disabilities begin speaking out on their own. Bowe and his supporters insisted that the UN should select a name to reflect the fact that people with disabilities were in control. In the end, 1981 was designated the International Year of Disabled Persons (IYDP).

People with disabilities always have played an important role in rehabilitation and special education programs. But these programs generally have been run by people who are not disabled. These nondisabled people may have had good intentions, but they did not always understand the needs and potential of the people they meant to serve. All too often they treated people with disabilities in a condescending manner, as if they were inferior beings.

The rehabilitation ("rehab") system is one example of a program *for* the disabled. Rehab agencies were created to teach people with disabilities new ways of performing such daily activities as dressing and cooking. They were also

Disability rights activists gather at the United Nations headquarters to hear discussion on the International Year of Disabled Persons.

meant to provide training so that disabled people could obtain jobs. Rehab agencies can purchase special equipment such as motorized wheelchairs, hearing aids, or computers with Braille displays for their clients. They may also pay a client's tuition at a trade school or college. To carry out these programs, most rehab agencies receive a combination of state and federal funding.

Over the years, some rehab agencies have become overrun by rules and regulations. To receive help, a disabled person must fill out endless forms and spend weeks or months on a waiting list. When training for a job is discussed at last, the client's hopes often are stifled. "You have to be realistic," the counselor might explain. "A blind person can't run a business. There's just too much bookkeeping. Why don't you become a typist instead?"

In part, the independent living movement grew out of the frustration disabled people felt with rehab programs and other agencies. These programs for the disabled were supposed to help them, but instead they often presented obstacles. At the centers for independent living (CILs), which sprang up in the 1970s, people with disabilities were in charge. They shared their experiences, pooled their resources, and helped one another reach their goals. These programs were not designed and staffed by outsiders who worked *for* the disabled.

They were *of* people with disabilities—created and controlled by disabled people themselves.

The words *for* and *of* are important in the names of many disability-related organizations. The American Foundation *for* the Blind (AFB) employs mostly sighted people and educates the public about blindness. It also sponsors research in areas that affect blind people. On the other hand, most members of the National Federation *of* the Blind (NFB) are blind people. Like the AFB, the NFB tries to educate the public about the abilities of blind people. It also does extensive advocacy work, helping blind people fight discrimination.

Groups such as the NFB are sometimes called consumer organizations. They are comprised of people who use, or consume, disability-related services, such as rehabilitation or health care. Other consumer organizations include the National Association of the Deaf (NAD), Mental Patients Liberation Front (MPLF), and Little People of America—an organization of persons of short stature.

Some consumer organizations sponsor social activities, such as dances and picnics. They may offer support groups, giving members the chance to share their experiences. Sometimes they publish literature to further the understanding of a particular disability. These groups often conduct political lobbying,

Members of the National Federation of the Blind stage a protest over an airline's seating policy for blind people.

seeking the support of legislators on disability-related issues. Working with government like this is called political advocacy, and it is an important function of many consumer groups. It is easier for a disabled person to fight discrimination when she or he has an organization's firm backing.

Some consumer groups focus upon a specific issue and work to bring about change. One of the best-known and most controversial consumer groups in the disability rights movement is ADAPT. When ADAPT was founded in 1983, the name stood for American Disabled for Accessible Public Transit. By staging protests around the country, ADAPT members fought for public transit systems to equip their buses with lifts to accommodate people who use wheelchairs. Protesters blocked traffic at bus stops in order to get their point across. Dozens were arrested. As ADAPT organizer Mark Johnson put it, "Black people fought for the right to ride at the front of the bus. We're fighting for the right to get on the bus." When the Americans with Disabilities Act (ADA) was passed in 1990, it required that all public transportation should be wheelchair-accessible by the year 2010.

In the 1990s, ADAPT changed its focus and its name. The familiar acronym ADAPT came to stand for Americans with Disabilities for Attendant Programs Today. Millions of disabled people need help with dressing, bathing, eating, using the bathroom, and other daily activities. Many of these people are forced to live in nursing homes in order to get the help they require. If they could hire attendants (people to help them at home), many of these men and women could live on their own. State and federal Medicaid funds will pay for nursing-home care but will not usually cover personal assistance for people living at home. ADAPT launched a fight to change the rules so that Medicaid money could be used for personal assistance as well as nursing-home care.

One of the most prominent disability-related organizations in the world is the Muscular Dystrophy Association (MDA). The MDA includes neither *for* nor *of* in its name, yet an ongoing debate cuts to the core of this issue. Founded in 1950, the MDA helps promote research into the cause and treatment of mus-

ADAPT protesters enter the U.S. Capitol in Washington, D.C.

cular dystrophy and some forty similar diseases. Every year over Labor Day weekend, the MDA sponsors a nationally televised telethon to raise funds. The telethon is sponsored by some of the nation's leading corporations and features guest appearances by top entertainers. Since 1966, the master of ceremonies has been actor Jerry Lewis, who is also chairman of the MDA. As Lewis asks viewers to phone in their pledges, he speaks of his dream that a cure will be found for "his kids." "Jerry's Kids," as the MDA calls them, are children disabled by muscular dystrophy. Spearheaded by Lewis's efforts, the MDA telethon has become perhaps the most recognizable disability-related event in the nation. It draws an audience of more than 120 million viewers. Financed by donations from many of those viewers, the MDA has been a leader in providing assistance for people with disabilities. And with the help of grants from the MDA, scientists have found a gene that is responsible for Duchenne muscular dystrophy, the most common form of the disease. Finding this critical gene is possibly the first step toward discovering an effective treatment.

As the years have passed, however, people with disabilities have grown dismayed with the MDA's fundraising approach. While some people believe the telethon is a wonderful opportunity to educate the public about muscular dystrophy, others are angry. The program focuses on tragic children who never will walk unless a cure is found. Some people feel that in his heartfelt pleas for money, Jerry Lewis implies that a life spent in a wheelchair is meaningless. Critics are concerned because the MDA's style of being an advocate *for* people with disabilities is to pity them and treat them as helpless children. The term "Jerry's Kids" implies that these people have no families of their own, and that they are utterly reliant on Jerry Lewis. Critics believe the MDA telethon leaves millions of viewers with the misconception that life in a wheelchair is pointless and endlessly painful. While thousands of disabled people embrace the MDA for the services and research it has provided, many other angry people continue to speak out against it.

Jerry Lewis with an MDA "poster child." Lewis and the Muscular Dystrophy Association have been criticized for the image they present of people with disabilities.

According to statistics, about forty million Americans—one of every seven—has some form of disability. But the disability rights movement is hardly a single, united force. Disabling conditions range from blindness to quadriplegia, from stuttering to diabetes, from mild to profound mental retardation. Some people have two or more disabilities. Some people with disabling conditions do not regard themselves as disabled at all.

Each disability presents its own, unique perspective, and people with one disability may have little understanding of those with another disability. Consumer groups built around a particular disability, such as deafness, blindness, or epilepsy, usually concentrate on the specific issues in the lives of those who have that condition. Organizations of people who use wheelchairs fight to eliminate architectural barriers. Groups such as the Mental Patients Liberation Front battle to change the laws regarding involuntary commitment of people with mental illnesses to hospitals. Groups of people who are blind work to promote the use of Braille. Sometimes these diverse organizations seem to have nothing in common, and even to be at odds with one another. Yet, when Congress was debating the Americans with Disabilities Act (ADA), some 180 groups for and of people with disabilities campaigned for the bill's passage. For almost the first time in history, people with disabilities combined their strength to promote a cause of importance to all of them. Despite the vast differences among disabilities, most disability rights leaders recognize the need for solidarity. They urge people with disabilities to join forces, to speak out for themselves and for others.

TEMPLE GRANDIN

1947–

Livestock-Handling Equipment Designer

When Temple Grandin was six months old, her mother noticed that she no longer enjoyed being cuddled. As the weeks passed, Temple fought her mother's touch, screaming and clawing. At first, Temple's mother thought this was a normal reaction in her growing child. But she quickly realized that her daughter did not act like other children her age. As time passed, she grew alarmed. Although Temple seemed to understand what others said to her, she did not speak. The sound of a car horn or a bursting paper bag made her scream as though she were in pain. Yet at other times, she did not seem to hear at all. And Temple could not bear to be touched. Not even her own mother could hug her.

When Temple was three, her parents took her to a neurologist, an expert on diseases of the nervous system. After a series of tests, the doctor concluded that Temple had a form of autism. People with autism have trouble processing the information that comes to them through the senses. They may overreact to sounds, smells, or touch. Often they deal with this "sensory overload" by withdrawing from the world around them. The neurologist who examined Temple recommended speech therapy and urged her parents to treat her as normally as possible.

It was not always easy to treat Temple like any normal child. She often was destructive and had violent tantrums. She had little interest in playing with other children. At the beach she sat for hours sifting sand between her fingers, seemingly oblivious to anything else. Her mother wrote in her diary, "My beautiful child—when she is good she is very, very good, and when she is bad she is horrid! . . . I must say, though, that even on her worst days she is intelligent and exciting. Temple is fun to be with and a dear companion."

At five, Temple entered kindergarten in a small private school. She could speak in only one- or two-word sentences, her coordination was poor, but she was extremely creative. When she did not have a pet to bring to the school's pet show, she brought herself; all day she acted the part of a dog, sitting up, barking, and begging for food.

For Temple, human touch was frightening and overwhelming. If someone hugged her, she felt as if she were going to suffocate. Yet she longed for the comfort that only touch can provide. When she was in second grade, she began to imagine a special "hugging machine." She pictured herself crawling into a long, narrow box with an inflatable lining that would hold her in its gentle embrace.

As she grew older, Temple struggled to make friends and to control her temper. Other children considered her odd, and many teased her cruelly. When she was in eighth grade, she was expelled from school for throwing a book at a girl who called her a "retard." Her mother searched for a school where Temple would have the chance to develop to her fullest potential. She found the ideal setting in Vermont at Mountain Country School, a boarding school for gifted children with emotional problems. The students were respected as individuals and were taught to respect themselves and one another.

At Mountain Country School, Temple got into fewer fights, but she began to have severe panic attacks when she was under stress. With autism, stress could be something as ordinary as a fire drill or an overly noisy class. Her heart raced, her palms sweated, and she felt as though she would faint. The thought of the future, when she would have to leave the safety of the school for the unfamiliar world outside, threw Temple into torments of fear.

One day during chapel service, the minister declared, "Before each of you there is a door into heaven. Open it and be saved." The words seized Temple's imagination. Her autism made it hard for her to understand abstract symbols. She thought the minister was describing an actual door, somewhere on the school campus, which would lead her to peace. For days she searched, trying one door after another. At last, she discovered the door to a tiny observation room on the roof of one of the classroom buildings. Stepping through it, she stood in a small, glassed-in enclosure, gazing out at the woods and mountains. "A feeling of relief flooded me," she wrote later. "For the first time in months I felt safe in the present and had hope for the future. A feeling of love and joy enveloped me. I'd found it! The door to my heaven." For Temple, the door represented growing up, passing from high school to the world beyond.

One summer while Temple was in high school, she visited her Aunt Anne on a ranch in Arizona. Temple became intrigued by the squeeze chute, a mechanical device that held the cows still for branding and inoculations. One by one, each cow was led into the chute and the sides were tightened around it, holding it fast. Terrified cows quickly grew calm under this firm but gentle pressure. Perhaps this was the "hugging machine" Temple had wished for long ago.

With some difficulty, Temple persuaded her aunt to let her get into the cattle chute. "The effect was both stimulating and relaxing at the same time," she recalled. "But most importantly for an autistic person, I was in control." Perhaps this machine could reduce her panic attacks and teach her to accept physical touch from other people.

Back at school, Temple threw herself into building a squeeze chute of her own. She spent every spare moment on the project, designing the device so that she could lock herself in, control the amount of pressure, and release herself at will. She could talk of nothing else. Her teachers thought her new obsession was bizarre and unhealthy. They told her parents to discourage her from using or even discussing the squeeze machine.

No matter how others objected, Temple did not give up her project. She knew that the machine was helping her to relax, to face situations that previously had been intolerable. She wanted to know why the machine's gentle pressure calmed frightened cows and had the same effect upon her. If she could learn the answers, she could persuade others of the value of her machine.

After graduation, Temple Grandin enrolled at a small college in Vermont, where she majored in psychology. In her reading, she learned about sensory interaction. Research in this field had shown that the pressure of touch can affect auditory thresholds, the amount of sound that a person finds acceptable. Here was scientific evidence to explain the workings of her squeeze machine. In her diary she wrote: "Children have to be taught to be gentle. Since I missed out on this, I have to learn it now. The squeeze chute gives the feeling of being held, cuddled, and gently cradled in Mother's arms. This is hard to write down. Writing it down is a form of accepting the feeling."

In 1971, Temple Grandin entered a master's program in psychology at the University of Arizona. After two years, she switched her field of study to animal science. By the time she earned her degree, she had published several papers on livestock-handling equipment, and she had found many ways to improve standard cattle chutes. Later she went on to earn a doctorate in animal science from the University of Illinois. Today she teaches livestock management at Colorado State University in Fort Collins, Colorado. She travels throughout the world, giving lectures and helping to design livestock facilities. Her work emphasizes the humane treatment of animals, even when they are about to be slaughtered for food.

Over the years, Temple Grandin continued her quest to cope with autism. A medication called inipramine helped control her panic attacks and made it possible for her to deal with many once-terrifying situations. Gradually she learned to accept human touch—a handshake, a pat on the shoulder, even the jostling of a crowd. Yet she still is often baffled by the complexities in human relationships. She watches people carefully, trying to model her behavior on that of others. She describes herself as "an anthropologist on Mars," struggling to understand the minds of alien beings. Despite her struggles, however, she is convinced that autism has been a positive force in her life. In a lecture, she commented: "If I could snap my fingers and be non-autistic, I would not, because then I wouldn't be me. Autism is part of who I am." She is dismayed when scientists speak of eliminating the genes that cause autism. "If the genes that cause [this condition] were eliminated, there might be a terrible price to pay," she wrote in an article. "It is possible that persons with bits of these traits are more creative, or possibly even geniuses."

In addition to her work with animals, Temple Grandin speaks eloquently on the needs and abilities of people with autism. Research has confirmed that her "hugging machine" can help many children who have autism, hyperactivity, and other neurological conditions. In her autobiography, *Emergence: Labeled Autistic*, Temple Grandin concludes, "With the help and love of family and others, I have come a long way—a very, very long way. With my ability for visual thinking, I 'see' others labeled autistic gliding through their symbolic doors to their own successes."

JUDY HEUMANN

1947–

Assistant Secretary
of Education

As a small child playing on the sidewalks of Brooklyn, Judy Heumann seldom felt that she was different. She used a wheelchair while her friends got around by walking, but they all enjoyed the same games. Like the other children she knew, Judy looked forward to starting school. She was bewildered when the local principal refused to let her enroll. The principal insisted that a child like Judy did not belong in a regular classroom with "normal" pupils.

Judy spent the next three and a half years on "home instruction." Two or three times a week, a teacher came to her family's apartment to work with her. Meanwhile, her mother fought a long, fierce battle with the local school board. At last, midway through fourth grade, Judy was assigned to a special class for children with disabilities. Nearly all of the other children in the class had cerebral palsy. Judy was the only student who was disabled as the result of poliomyelitis, which she contracted when she was eighteen months old.

Judy loved meeting her new classmates. She formed a close-knit circle of friends who shared disability as a common bond. They were all painfully conscious that their class was segregated, a tiny island apart from the rest of the school. They had few chances to get to know the nondisabled students.

Furthermore, their teachers rarely pushed them to do their best. The teachers never seemed to expect very much from students who were disabled.

Judy had a similar experience when she went to a special summer camp for disabled children. She liked her fellow campers very much but wondered why they couldn't all go to camp with nondisabled children. And why weren't any of the counselors disabled? Though the camp tried to meet the needs of disabled children, it was run entirely by nondisabled people. Judy wished she could meet some adults with disabilities. She wanted to learn about their jobs, their families, their lives.

Soon after Judy entered the special class, her parents discovered that wheelchair users could not attend any of the local high schools. This meant that when she completed eighth grade, Judy would be forced to return to home instruction. Judy was still in sixth grade when her mother got to work. She organized a group of parents whose children had disabilities. With their united strength, the parents pressured the board of education to make a number of high-school programs accessible to disabled students. By the time Judy was ready for ninth grade, these programs were in place.

Judy Heumann recalls high school as a difficult period in her life. She had never been required to compete academically, and now she felt overwhelmed. The school had ramps and elevators, but she did not have a motorized wheelchair. Without help, she could not get from class to class. The school hired an aide to push her wheelchair. Since she always was shepherded by the aide, she became separated from the other students. In addition, the students with disabilities all were placed together in a special homeroom, so they were further isolated from their nondisabled classmates. Judy sensed that most nondisabled kids felt awkward in her company. They saw her as "the girl in the wheelchair," and not as a whole person.

Like most of her classmates, Judy was excited as graduation approached. She was to receive a special award for scholastic achievement at the graduation ceremony. But as her father prepared to lift her onto the stage, the principal rushed toward them. Judy could not sit on the stage, he insisted. He would bring the award to her seat in the front row of the auditorium. Judy tried not to cry. After all her years of struggle, she was being excluded once again. She wanted to give up and go home. But her father insisted that she take her rightful place on the stage, and at last the principal relented. Judy now reflects, "It was one more example of the discrimination disabled people face all the time. You never know when something like that is going to happen. It can hit you when you least expect it, and ruin some occasion you've planned for months. You never feel totally safe."

After high school, Judy Heumann entered Long Island University. Gradually she made friends and joined school activities. She tried out for plays and ran for student government. She also became involved with other disabled students on campus. Together they worked to make the university more accessible to people with disabilities. For years, Judy had observed as her parents fought for her rights. They had always challenged the limitations that outsiders tried to place upon her. Now she knew she had to fight for herself—and for others as well. "It wasn't enough just to study hard," she explains. "I knew that the American Dream didn't work for you if you were disabled. You had to fight for everything you wanted, every step of the way."

Though she had many friends at college, Judy Heumann rarely went out on dates. Most boys did not see her as interesting and attractive. One day a boy knocked on her door and asked if she knew any girl who might like to go out with his friend, who was visiting for the weekend. Clearly he did not think Judy herself was a possibility. His question made her feel as if she were invisible.

During college, Judy Heumann studied to become a teacher. Though she passed all of the required courses, she failed the New York City Board of Education's medical exam. A person who used a wheelchair was automatically disqualified from teaching in New York schools. Judy called the American Civil Liberties Union (ACLU), an organization that protects people's legal rights. She argued that the school board was discriminating against her because of her disability. The ACLU refused to help. Her case was not a matter of discrimination, she was told. She had been turned down for medical reasons.

The year was 1970. Looking back, Judy Heumann realized that she had been battling the New York City Board of Education for most of her life—first as a student, and now as a prospective teacher. She decided it was time to fight back. She contacted a reporter for the *New York Times,* and the paper ran a story about Judy's struggle. Within a few days, three lawyers offered to represent her in a lawsuit against the school board.

By starting her lawsuit, Judy Heumann went public as a disabled person fighting for her rights. The struggle was not for herself alone, but for all people with disabilities. Like African-Americans, disabled people had been oppressed for centuries. They had been taught to ask little from life, to be grateful for charity, to stay in their places. Judy Heumann decided she would work to bring that oppression to an end.

As the case gathered momentum, Judy Heumann made many public appearances. She was interviewed on the *Today* show. Articles about her ran in *Time* and *Good Housekeeping* magazines. At last the judge ruled that the school board must send her for a new medical examination. This time she passed. Even after she passed the physical, however, the school board refused to hire Judy Heumann. She continued to wage a war of publicity until she was finally offered a job. Ironically, she began her teaching career in a special class for children with disabilities—the very same class she had attended as a fourth-grader. She taught for the next three years, both special classes and regular second grade.

The publicity over her lawsuit brought Judy Heumann a flood of letters and phone calls, many of which came from others who had encountered job discrimination because of their disabilities. She listened to countless stories of shattered hopes and wasted lives. Somehow she had to bring these people together and find a way for them to fight the system that was holding them back.

In 1970, when she was twenty-two years old, Judy Heumann and several friends who had disabilities founded an organization called Disabled in Action (DIA). Eighty people arrived for DIA's first meeting. From the beginning, DIA had a political focus. In 1970, it was perfectly legal to discriminate against people with disabilities. They had no protection under civil rights laws. DIA set out to secure that protection in New York state and in the nation as a whole.

DIA lobbied legislators, published articles, and organized demonstrations. In 1972, President Richard Nixon vetoed a bill to fund expanded disability programs. DIA members joined a group of disabled veterans to protest at Nixon's New York City campaign headquarters. Later that year they demonstrated at the Lincoln Memorial in Washington, D.C.

In 1973, Judy Heumann moved to Berkeley, California, where she was swept into the rising independent-living movement, joining forces with Ed Roberts and other disability rights activists. To Judy, Berkeley was a revelation. It was a joy to cruise up and down ramps in her wheelchair, to use lift-equipped buses, to glide over curb cuts when she crossed the street. She could go wherever she wanted without restrictions. In Berkeley, people with disabilities had found a political voice; they were visible, they were speaking out, and they were changing the landscape. From 1975 until 1982, Judy Heumann served as deputy director of the Center for Independent Living (CIL) in Berkeley. The program provided peer counseling and other self-help services to people with disabilities. It also was a hub of political activity.

When Congress passed the new Rehabilitation Act in 1973, a part of the law called Section 504 made it illegal for any agency or institution that received federal funding to discriminate against a person or persons because of disability. Judy Heumann and other disability rights leaders were overjoyed. At last a federal law promised civil rights for disabled people. But for the next four years, Section 504 was not enforced. Its regulations had to be drawn up and signed by Joseph Califano, secretary of the Department of Health, Education, and Welfare (HEW). If Califano failed to sign, Section 504 would be forgotten.

Disability rights groups all over the country urged Califano to sign the Section 504 regulations. But he still did not sign the legislation. In response, activists staged a series of demonstrations. In April 1977, Judy Heumann led the takeover of the HEW offices in San Francisco. Hundreds of people with disabilities occupied the offices for twenty-six days. It was a time of enormous solidarity. People who were blind or deaf, who used wheelchairs, who had mental retardation or cerebral palsy, and those with a host of other disabling conditions gathered together in a common struggle for equality and independence. "We will not accept more segregation!" Judy Heumann told reporters. "There will be more sit-ins until the government understands this."

On April 28, 1977, Joseph Califano finally signed the Section 504 regulations into law. The demonstrators ended their vigil at the HEW offices. As news cameras flashed and reporters held out microphones, the protesters sang in triumph: "We have overcome!"

In 1983, with Ed Roberts, Judy Heumann cofounded the World Institute on Disability (WID) in Oakland, California. WID serves as a think tank on disability issues, a place where experts discuss new and old ideas. WID succeeded in bringing together researchers and policymakers to examine the issue of disability in such areas as health care, technology, housing, education, and employment.

On June 29, 1993, Judy Heumann was sworn in as assistant secretary of education under President Bill Clinton. This high-ranking government position put her in charge of the Office of Special Education and Rehabilitation Services (OSERS), where she manages an annual budget of more than $5.5 billion. Programs under OSERS serve some six million children and adults with disabilities. Judy Heumann sees OSERS as "working aggressively and collaboratively to create a society in which all disabled people can obtain the knowledge and skills necessary to achieve the goals they set for themselves."

Judy Heumann lives in Washington, D.C., where she keeps up with an impossibly busy schedule of meetings and interviews. In 1994, she married Jorge Pineda, an accountant. "I will feel I have accomplished my goal if we stop seeing the needs of disabled people as being special and different," she says, "[when] disabled people become integrated, productive members of our communities."

∞

1950–

Musician

When Steveland Morris was eight years old, he had a wonderful dream. He dreamed he had made a hit record, and it was playing on the radio. Bundles of money tumbled from the sky and piled up around him. Then he awoke to reality—an overcrowded apartment on the East Side of Detroit. No one who knew Stevie at that time could have imagined his dream coming true.

Steveland Morris was born several weeks prematurely. To save his life, doctors placed him in an incubator, where he received oxygen. At that time, no one knew that high doses of oxygen could damage a newborn baby's eyes. By the time Stevie was strong enough to go home, he was totally blind.

When Stevie was young, his parents divorced. His mother moved the family from Saginaw, Michigan, to Detroit, where she eventually remarried. She worked long hours in a fish-smoking plant, and Stevie's stepfather was a baker's assistant.

Stevie was a bright, active boy, who loved climbing trees and playing practical jokes. His true passion was music. When he was four, he started learning to play the piano. When his uncle gave him a harmonica, Stevie mastered the instrument almost overnight. He also enjoyed working out complicated rhythms on his toy drums. He pounded his way through several sets before a local Lions Club gave him some real drums for Christmas.

When he was nine, Stevie began singing solos at the Whitestone Baptist Church. One day, a church member heard him and his friends singing rock 'n' roll songs on the church steps. When the director of the choir found out, Stevie was expelled from the choir.

One of Stevie's friends had an older brother who played with a rhythm and blues band called the Miracles. When Stevie was ten, this musician friend took him to visit the recording studio at Motown Records. Stevie was thrilled. He began hanging around the studio after school, experimenting with various instruments and playing songs he had written himself. The managers at Motown were stunned by Stevie's talent, and they encouraged him to develop as a songwriter and performer. Years later, Stevie recalled, "Motown meant discipline to me. The attitude was 'Do it over, do it differently, do it until it can't be done any better.'"

Stevie worked hard. In 1963, Motown released his first hit single, "Fingertips, Part Two." It was an instant success. It sold a million copies, earning Stevie his first gold record. The piece was an instrumental composed by Stevie with Motown manager Ray Paul. Stevie dazzled his listeners with his performance on the harmonica. That summer, Motown brought out an album entitled *Little Stevie Wonder: The Twelve-Year-Old Genius.* From that time on, Steveland Morris had a new name—Stevie Wonder.

For the next few years, Stevie continued to attend public school, but he spent almost half his time on tour, performing at African-American nightclubs around the country. Motown Records acted as his guardian, holding his blockbuster earnings in trust for him until he turned twenty-one. Motown also controlled the kind of music Stevie produced.

During high school, Stevie Wonder enrolled at the Michigan School for the Blind in Lansing. After he graduated in 1969, he briefly studied composing

*Stevie Wonder
in the 1960s*

and musical arranging at the University of Southern California in Los Angeles. When working on arrangements, he used Braille music sheets.

After his first album, Stevie Wonder continued to produce a string of hit songs, including "Uptight," "I Was Made to Love Her," and "For Once in My Life." In the late 1960s, Motown dropped the "Little" from his name. By then, Stevie Wonder stood more than six feet tall.

At first, Stevie Wonder appealed to mostly African-American audiences. But by the late 1960s, he had won a large white following, as well, becoming one of pop music's first "crossover" artists who was popular among different audiences. After a performance in Manhattan, the *New York Post* called him "an honest prodigy of flawless taste and superb talent. He is not a singer, but he is one of the world's virtuosos on the chromatic harmonica."

In 1971, Stevie Wonder turned twenty-one. For a long time, he had been frustrated by Motown's control over his life. He decided to break with the company and strike out on his own. With a million-dollar investment, he opened his own recording studio. There he developed many of the musical ideas that he had been storing up for years. For the first time, he experimented with computerized instruments called music synthesizers. His first self-produced album, *Music of My Mind*, explored new realms of melody, rhythm, and harmony. He performed most of the vocals and played most of the instruments himself.

The following year, Stevie Wonder returned to Motown under a new contract that allowed him greater artistic freedom. His next album, *Talking Book* (with an album cover featuring both print and Braille writing), was one of his biggest hits. One reviewer exclaimed, "[It is] the most mature, though not the most accessible, album to date by a prodigious figure in popular music."

In the summer of 1973, Stevie Wonder was in a serious automobile accident in North Carolina. He was in a coma for a week. But after nearly two months in the hospital, he made a full recovery. In January 1974, he was nominated for six Grammy Awards. No other musician had ever received so many nominations at once. When the awards were handed out in March, he won five Grammies, including Best Vocal Performance by a Male Singer for his song "You Are the Sunshine of My Life." His album *Inner Visions* won the award for Best Album of the Year.

In the early 1970s, Stevie Wonder often produced two to three albums in a single year. As the decade drew to a close, his output began to slow down. Sometimes as much as two years passed between records, and some of his new work met a lukewarm reception from fans and critics. His 1979 album *Journey Through the Secret Life of Plants* was once nicknamed "Shrubbish."

During the 1980s, Wonder used his high profile to champion causes that were important to him. He joined the campaign to have Dr. Martin Luther King Jr.'s birthday declared a national holiday. He also worked to pressure South Africa to end its apartheid policy of rigid racial separation.

By the 1990s, Stevie Wonder seemed to be living on his past glory as a musician. But in 1995 he delighted audiences with a fresh new album, *Conversation Piece*. Stevie Wonder has been deeply religious all his life, and this album reflects his spiritual leanings. The opening song is a fervent prayer, "Rain Your Love Down." "I'm new with every song I sing," he explains. "As we get older, we feel the need for newness. I'm going to be forty-five, but I still feel new and amazed by the world I live in."

JOHN CALLAHAN

1951–

Cartoonist and Activist

A man leaves the refreshment stand at a baseball game and slips on a banana peel. He sprawls to the ground, spilling his popcorn, fries, soda, and hot dog. The caption reads: "What kind of a God would allow a thing like this to happen?"

This is just one typical cartoon from the pen of John Callahan. As a reviewer put it, "Callahan captures the essence of our stupidity, selfishness, and lack of feeling for others, and makes us laugh because we take it all so seriously." He finds rich humor in situations that make most people uncomfortable.

Many of Callahan's cartoons view ordinary situations from a disabled person's perspective. In a series of cartoon strips called "How to Relate to Handicapped People," he spoofs the awkwardness many people feel when meeting a person with a disability. By making people laugh at themselves, Callahan helps them overcome their uneasiness. Through humor, he challenges existing attitudes toward the disabled. Not all of John Callahan's cartoons are about living with disabilities. He pokes fun at doctors and lawyers, criminals and cops, movie stars, politicians, and bureaucrats. But the subject of disability is especially important to him. Callahan has been a quadriplegic since he was twenty-one years old.

John Callahan was born on February 5, 1951, at Saint Vincent's Hospital in Portland, Oregon. When he was six months old, he was adopted by a young, Irish-Catholic couple, David and Rosemary Callahan. The Callahan family soon moved to The Dalles, Oregon, where John would spend most of his youth.

John was the eldest of six children. Although he had three brothers and two sisters, he spent much of his time alone in the family library. While the other Callahan children enjoyed athletic games, John preferred to read, draw, and write poetry. John's elementary-school years were spent at Saint Mary's Academy. He was a good enough student that he sometimes tutored other children in his class. Callahan has always had a mischievous streak, however, and by the time he reached the fourth grade, he was well known for his cartoons. His drawings were very popular with other students, but his teachers were not always amused.

After graduating from Saint Mary's, John entered a public high school. His high-school classes were not as challenging as those at Saint Mary's had been, and John began to neglect his studies. He also started drinking alcohol, a habit he could not break for many years. After graduating from high school, Callahan drifted from job to job, growing steadily more depressed.

At twenty-one, hoping to leave his unhappiness and his alcoholism behind him, John Callahan moved to California. Soon after the move, his life was changed forever. On July 9, 1972, he was the passenger in a car that swerved off the road and into a utility pole. The driver was not badly hurt, but Callahan's spinal cord was severed. Doctors told the young man that the injury had occurred very high on his spine. This meant that he would have no use of his legs and very little use of his arms and hands. He spent almost a year in hospitals and rehabilitation centers.

For several years after the accident, John Callahan felt unhappy and purposeless. When he was twenty-seven years old, he finally realized that his problems were due to his dependence on alcohol, and not to his quadriplegia. He joined Alcoholics Anonymous and began attending college classes at Portland

State University. He also rediscovered his artistic talent. Callahan's cartoons began to appear in the student newspaper at Portland State University. At last, he knew what he wanted to do with his life.

Callahan graduated from college when he was thirty-one years old. Later that year, one of his cartoons was accepted by a national magazine. Since then, his work has been printed in *Omni, New Yorker, National Lampoon,* and many other leading periodicals. Callahan has published several collections of cartoons, including *Do Not Disturb Any Further,* and an autobiography called *Don't Worry, He Won't Get Far on Foot!* His book *The King of Things and the Cranberry Clown* is a fable in rhyme about a king who ties strings to each of his subjects in order to keep everyone under his control.

John Callahan is no longer the confused, depressed man who moved to California in the summer of 1972. Today, he is a successful cartoonist who is justly proud of his accomplishments. In addition, he has become an activist for the rights of people with disabilities. "I feel I have a special calling," he explains. "When I do the work I was born to do, I get a sense of fulfillment that keeps me going. I see reasons for the things I've lived through."

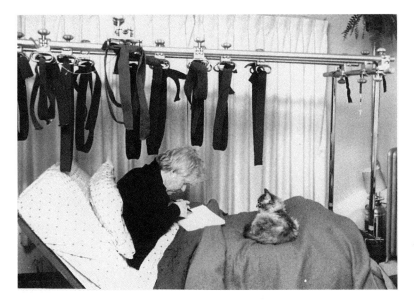

In his bed, John Callahan creates cartoons that poke fun at people's attitudes about disability.

The Right to Live, The Right to Die

❧

"At least I wasn't part of the killing," said Linda McCabe, a nurse at Bloomington Hospital in Indiana. "The other nurses in Special Care and I told the hospital administration we would not help starve that child. So the baby was moved to another part of the hospital, and the parents had to hire private nurses."

Linda McCabe was one of the first nurses assigned to care for an infant that reporters called "Baby Doe." Baby Doe was born with a blockage in his esophagus. The condition required immediate surgery if he was to survive. But because the baby also had Down syndrome, his parents and doctors decided that he should not have the lifesaving operation. If he lived, they believed, he would never have "a minimally adequate quality of life." They felt it would be best to let the baby die.

The doctors ordered that Baby Doe should be given no food or water. Then he began the slow process of starving to death. Outraged by the events, Linda McCabe and several other nurses alerted the media. Disability rights activists tried to get the courts to intervene and place Baby Doe back on food and water. Several families offered to adopt the baby, but his parents refused. They explained that if he was allowed to live, they believed their child could lead a life only of suffering and misery. They thought he would be better off dead. After six long days, Baby Doe died on April 15, 1982.

The Baby Doe case sparked a nationwide controversy. Many people—especially doctors and hospital administrators—felt that parents and physicians, alone, should decide whether severely disabled infants received medical treatment. Such decisions, they insisted, were very private matters, to be kept out of the newspapers and courtrooms. Other people, particularly disability rights

Protesters object to the killing of "Baby Doe" in 1982.

activists, argued that Baby Doe had died because of prejudice against people with disabilities. With the proper education and support, people with Down syndrome live fulfilling and happy lives. Baby Doe's parents and doctors passed judgment on the value of his life when he was born. He had no one else to speak on his behalf.

What happened to Baby Doe was not unique. In 1973, an article in the prestigious *New England Journal of Medicine* described the withholding of food and surgery as a "treatment option" for babies with Down syndrome, spina bifida, cerebral palsy, and other disabilities. It referred to the "success" of this "option" in forty-three cases. The doctors who wrote the article claimed that these babies would have grown up to be "vegetables."

For decades, doctors had quietly counseled parents to let their disabled newborns die "for the good of everyone concerned." The practice wasn't exactly legal, but it was rarely challenged. No one knows how many agonized parents followed this medical advice. But some families refused to accept death as the best answer for their children. They fought for treatment, for education, for rehabilitation, and gave their disabled sons and daughters the best possible start in life. Among people with disabilities, the same story is heard again and again: "The doctors told my parents to give up and let me die. But my family took me home anyway, and here I am!"

After reading the article in the *New England Journal of Medicine*, a psychologist named Sondra Diamond wrote to *Newsweek* magazine. "I'll wager my entire root system and as much fertilizer as it would take to fill Yale University that you have never received a letter from a vegetable before this one. But, much as I resent the term, I must confess that I fit the description of a vegetable as defined in the [journal] article. Due to severe brain damage incurred at birth, I am unable to dress myself, toilet myself, or write myself. My secretary is typing this letter. . . . My parents were told . . . that there was little or no hope of achieving meaningful humanhood for their daughter, afflicted with cerebral palsy. . . . Instead of changing the law to make it legal to weed out us vegetables, let us change the law so that we may receive quality medical care, education, and freedom to live as full and productive lives as our potentials allow."

The Baby Doe case came at a time when disabled persons were becoming a political force in the United States. Section 504 of the Rehabilitation Act of 1973 stated that no program receiving federal funds could discriminate against people with disabilities. Hospitals received federal funds, and the refusal to treat a disabled infant was seen as discrimination against those infants. Supported by Section 504, President Ronald Reagan ordered that infants with disabilities must be fed and given treatment like any others. Then, in 1984, Congress amended federal child-abuse legislation to cover disabled infants. Today, the withholding of food or treatment from a disabled child is an act of abuse under the law.

Babies who have disabilities cannot speak for themselves. For them, life and death decisions must rest in the hands of parents, doctors, and the courts. For adults with disabilities, however, the situation is different. Disabled adults usually can express themselves and make their wishes known. At times, people with severe disabilities have asked friends, relatives, and the courts to help them die.

In 1989, a Georgia man named Larry McAfee asked his physician to help him commit suicide. McAfee was a quadriplegic who breathed with the help of a machine called a respirator. He spent every day at home with his parents, feeling utterly bored, isolated, and hopeless. He wanted to be given sedatives, and then to have his respirator turned off. He said he would rather die than go on living in misery.

When Larry McAfee's story appeared in the newspapers, he was contacted by several quadriplegics who used respirators. Some of them had jobs; some were married; most lived on their own with the help of personal-care assistants. They showed McAfee that he could make friends, that his life could still be interesting and meaningful. After getting to know these active, self-confident people with disabilities, Larry McAfee began to believe that he did not want to give up and die. With the help of a center for independent living, he moved into a house with four other disabled people. He hired attendants to help him with dressing, eating, and going to the bathroom, and he began to think about college.

If a nondisabled person talks about committing suicide, most people react with concern. Friends and family usually try to show him or her that life is still worth living; therapists and counselors attempt to treat the person for severe depression. When a person with a disability announces that she or he wants to die, the response is often very different. Most people assume that life with a severe disability is intolerable. Therefore they conclude that the disabled person is making a rational choice. Disability rights activists argue that most disabled people would choose to live if only they had personal assistance and other needed supports in the community. They contend that persons with disabilities and their families should explore all of the possibilities for independent living before making such an enormous decision.

The "right to die" issue leaped into the headlines in June 1990, when a Michigan doctor named Jack Kevorkian assisted in the suicide of fifty-four-year-old Janet Adkins. Janet Adkins was in the early stages of Alzheimer's disease. She knew that she would gradually lose her memory and her ability to think clearly. Her body would deteriorate, as well, until she could no longer walk or feed herself. Rather than subject herself and her loved ones to this long and painful death, she ended her own life quickly and painlessly with the help of Dr. Kevorkian. In the years that followed, Kevorkian assisted in the suicide deaths of several other disabled and chronically ill people. Because of their disabilities, most of these people could not have committed suicide without help from another person.

Kevorkian claimed that he was acting out of compassion, aiding people to escape lives of helplessness and pain. The public's reaction was mixed. Many people were horrified by these "assisted suicides." But others felt that Kevorkian was performing a work of mercy. Public officials and private citizens murmured, "If I were ever bedridden like that, I'd want to kill myself, too."

Most disability rights activists believed that Kevorkian's actions sprang from prejudice and misperceptions. Why, they asked, doesn't society take measures to make life more livable for disabled people? Why does death seem to be the logical solution for people with disabilities when they are in despair? The disability rights movement has worked hard to give disabled people a sense of self-worth. "Right to die" cases can threaten the idea that life with a disability is still meaningful and valuable.

The issues around the right to die are highly personal and complex. An individual's decision is based on his or her circumstances, and each person's situation is unique. What is acceptable to one person may be unbearable to someone else.

Julie Reiskin has multiple sclerosis (MS), a disease that causes the progressive destruction of the body's nervous system. A person with MS may become more and more severely disabled as time passes. Reiskin explains that most people with progressive diseases have their "line." By a "line," she means the level of disability at which you believe you could not continue living. "Three years ago my line lay at not being able to run," Reiskin writes. "Then it moved to not being able to climb the stairs. It moved again, to not being able to walk, then to not being able to drive. Seeing as how I am writing this and I can no longer do any of these things, it's clear I've changed my line again." Reiskin's line had

Dr. Jack Kevorkian

shifted steadily, and she adjusted to each change in her condition. Yet she believed that someday she might no longer be able or willing to adjust any further. She might reach her final line, at last.

The disability rights movement seeks to enhance the quality of life for disabled people, to make living with a disability worthwhile. On a deeper level, the movement tries to empower people with disabilities, to give them the freedom to shape their own destinies. At times, taking control of one's life may mean deciding when that life should come to a close. Julie Reiskin speaks for many disabled people when she insists that the individual must have the right to make the ultimate decision. "Making room for people to die in the community is as much a disability issue as demanding that we be allowed to live in the community," Reiskin states. "Those of us with progressive illnesses need support, regardless of our choices."

SUSAN NUSSBAUM

⌒

1953–

Actor, Playwright

W hen the Goodman Theater in Chicago decided to stage the play *She Always Said Pablo* in 1987, the director asked Susan Nussbaum to audition. Assuming that she would be auditioning for a part in the chorus, she agreed. To her delight, the director selected her for the leading role, that of the writer Gertrude Stein. Like any actor, Nussbaum hungered for a starring role in a full-scale production. But in addition, this role was a very special opportunity—it was her first opportunity to play a major part that was not written specifically for a person with a disability.

As a child growing up in Chicago, Susan Nussbaum always knew that she wanted to act. But whenever a school play came along, she felt too shy to try out for a part. Nevertheless, her parents encouraged her ambitions. Susan's father, Mike Nussbaum, was especially sympathetic. He, too, had long dreamed of a theater career. When Susan was in her teens, her father left his job as an exterminator to become a professional actor.

While Susan was in high school, she and some classmates wrote and produced a play about women's liberation. Since she had worked on the script, Susan was able to take an acting part without the ordeal of a tryout. She saw the play as a means of making an important political statement. The school, however, took a dim view of the entire production because the play included a graphic description of an abortion. Susan Nussbaum was suspended from school. Fortunately for her, her parents were very supportive. They respected her commitment to her ideals.

After high school, Susan studied theater arts at the Goodman School of Drama, which was affiliated with the Art Institute of Chicago. In 1978, when she was almost ready to graduate, she was struck by a car on her way to class. The accident fractured her spine, and she became a quadriplegic.

For a long time, Susan was convinced that her life was over. She felt shell-shocked, appalled by the changes in her body. She saw herself as defective, a person who could never fit into the world of "normal" people. She could not imagine working, dating, or living independently again.

Susan spent several months at the Rehabilitation Institute in Chicago. Shortly before she returned home, she received a call from a man who produced radio dramas. He knew her father and had heard about her injury. He wanted to offer her a job doing office work.

At first, Susan found the work unbearably hard. She had very little use of her hands, so even filing papers and answering the telephone were a challenge. But she found the atmosphere at the studio comfortable and relaxed. The people on the staff were bright and witty, and they accepted her as one of them. Soon she was taking roles in radio dramas, thrilled to be acting again.

Though she loved her job, Susan Nussbaum was still deeply depressed. At night, she sat alone in her apartment, feeling isolated and lost. She felt as though no one could understand what her life was like, as if she were alone in all the world.

After eighteen months at the radio job, Susan learned of a new program in Chicago called Access Living. It was run by people with disabilities who were finding innovative ways to help one another. When Susan visited Access Living, she entered a new world. Suddenly she was surrounded by people who shared her experience, who understood her fears and frustrations. They were people with disabilities who lived full and rewarding lives. For the first time since her accident, Susan did not feel separated from society. She realized that she, too, could build the life she had always wanted.

Susan Nussbaum left her job at the radio station and began to work part-time at Access Living. Her involvement transformed her thinking about disability. She saw disabled people not as inferior beings, but as a minority group faced with discrimination. She found that disabled people shared a unique perspective on life, and even had a special brand of humor all their own.

Her passion for the theater and her awareness of disability humor led Susan Nussbaum to write her first play, *Staring Back*. Cowritten with Larry Perkins, *Staring Back* is a series of humorous sketches. The play pokes fun at the public's many misconceptions about people with disabilities. Most of the actors in the production had disabilities, including blindness, deafness, and spinal-cord injury. Susan Nussbaum acted in several of the skits. In 1984, *Staring Back* opened at Chicago's comedy revue theater, Second City, and went on to win awards and praise from audiences and critics alike.

Susan Nussbaum has written six plays, each in some way related to disability issues. Her plays include *Telethon*, *The Plucky and Spunky Show*, and *Mishuganismo*. Susan Nussbaum teaches drama, directs plays, and continues to act. In the theater, disability usually has been treated as a tragedy. Playwrights have long used disabled characters to arouse pity or fear. Susan Nussbaum's work helps to unravel ancient stereotypes. She gives the audience permission to laugh as well as cry.

JOHN HOCKENBERRY

1956–

Journalist

On a bright February day in 1976, John Hockenberry and a friend stood beside a highway in central Pennsylvania. Two girls stopped to give them a lift. For a while, the four young people talked and laughed together. Then, as John dozed in the back seat, the driver fell asleep at the wheel. John snapped awake as the car hurtled off the road and down a steep embankment. As soon as he realized what had happened, he noticed that he had no feeling in his legs and feet. Sitting in the twisted wreck, waiting for help, he knew that his back was broken. He knew he would never be able to walk again.

John Hockenberry grew up in Binghamton, New York. Looking back, he describes himself as "a science nerd, a complete klutz" as a teenager. His first love was music, and he spent long, happy hours practicing the guitar. In 1975, he entered the University of Chicago as a mathematics major. He had just finished his first semester at the time of his automobile accident.

John spent several months at a rehabilitation institute in Pennsylvania. A rigorous exercise program strengthened his arms and shoulders so that he could swing in and out of his wheelchair. Because of the damage to his spinal cord, he could no longer urinate in the usual way. Nurses taught him to empty his bladder by using a flexible plastic tube called a catheter. Visitors often remarked that John was adjusting remarkably well to his disability. Some asked if he had considered committing suicide, convinced that he must be in despair. "Far from being a blank wall of misery, my body now presented an intriguing puzzle of great depth and texture," he explained years later. "My body may have been capable of less, but virtually all of what it could do was suddenly charged with meaning. This feeling was the hardest to translate to the outside, where people wanted to believe that I must have to paint things in this way to keep from killing myself."

In the long, level corridors of the rehab center, John glided swiftly and gracefully in his wheelchair. But life back home was cluttered with stairs, narrow doorways, and an overabundance of tables and chairs. A visit to a friend's house or an outing to the movies required endless maneuvering. John never doubted that the extra effort was worthwhile. He was willing to do whatever was necessary, as long as he could pick up his life where it had left off.

That fall, John Hockenberry returned to the University of Chicago. Only two of the classroom buildings on campus were accessible to a person who used a wheelchair. He was forced to ask his professors to move their classes to buildings he could enter. Some were happy to cooperate. Others let him know that he was putting them to a great deal of extra trouble. When winter came, the sidewalks were impassable with mounds of snow. Eventually John left Chicago for the University of Oregon in Eugene. Oregon winters were mild, and most of the Eugene campus was wheelchair accessible.

John Hockenberry enrolled at the University of Oregon as a music major. For two years, he concentrated on the piano and harpsichord. Then, in 1980, he volunteered at KLCC, a campus station affiliated with National Public Radio (NPR). In addition to running news programs produced by NPR, KLCC also produced "alternative radio" programs of its own—eight- and ten-part series on such topics as nuclear waste and endangered species.

In May 1980, Mount St. Helens volcano erupted in Washington State.

With the nation's attention focused on the Pacific Northwest, NPR dispatched a reporter to KLCC to follow the story. John Hockenberry worked on these reports, and in the following months, began preparing his own reports for NPR on other issues in Washington and Oregon. For one report, Hockenberry stayed up all night working on the story, though the piece would run in just a sixty-second slot on NPR. When he telephoned the piece to NPR, he talked fast to fit everything in. Later his mother told him, "Your father and I heard you say your name. But what was the story about?"

Over the months that followed, NPR sent John Hockenberry to cover many more regional news events. Because he was submitting reports by voice, nobody at NPR headquarters in Washington, D.C., had ever seen him. Nobody knew that he used a wheelchair. Hockenberry reveled in the knowledge that he was being judged on the basis of his work alone. No one at NPR gushed over his achievements; no one questioned whether he could get a job done either.

One day, working on a story in rural Washington, Hockenberry could not find a wheelchair-accessible pay phone. His deadline drew closer and closer, and he had no way to send in his report. By the time he found a phone he could use, he had missed his five-o'clock deadline. He had to explain what had happened, and the secret finally was out. In his entire career, this was the only time Hockenberry ever missed a deadline.

In 1981, Hockenberry left college and moved to Washington, D.C., to take a full-time job with NPR. For the next three years, he worked as a newscaster on public radio's evening program, *All Things Considered.* He prepared quick summaries of the major news stories that came over the wires, delivering them on the air to a nationwide audience. But he preferred on-the-scene reporting, so in 1984, he requested a transfer. NPR sent him to its Chicago bureau, where he spent the next four years covering stories all over the Midwest.

John Hockenberry set out on his first foreign assignment in 1988. Stationed in Jerusalem, he reported for two years on the tensions between Israel and the Palestine Liberation Organization (PLO). Hockenberry found it very difficult to get around in Jerusalem. The city had few ramped curbs, and its sidewalks were often broken by twisting flights of stairs. With ingenuity and perseverance, and by overcoming his dread of asking for help, Hockenberry made his way through the troubled city. He formed lasting friendships with both Israelis and Palestinians, and his stories on NPR explored both sides of the conflict. Hockenberry returned to Israel in 1991 to report on the Persian Gulf War. When the fighting ended, he traveled to northern Iraq. On the back of a donkey, he climbed treacherous mountain trails to report on the plight of Kurdish refugees.

John Hockenberry left NPR in 1992 for a job with the ABC television network, where he worked as a correspondent with the ABC news magazine *Day One*. In 1995, he switched to CNBC, and in 1996, he joined NBC news as a reporter.

John Hockenberry brings a rare creativity and sense of compassion to his news reporting. These traits reflect the way in which he lives his life. "From the beginning, disability taught me that life could be reinvented," he explains. "The physical dimensions of life could be created, like poetry; they were not imposed by some celestial landlord. . . . [To the people who stared] I was getting by in dealing with my predicament. To them, I was standing on a ledge and not jumping off. To me, I was climbing up to get a better view."

TOM CRUISE

1962–

Actor

Hollywood film producer once remarked about Tom Cruise that "guys want to be like him and girls want to be with him." Cruise vaulted to stardom in the mid-1980s with roles in such box-office hits as *Risky Business*, *The Color of Money*, and *Top Gun*. Frequently he plays a toughened street survivor with a charming streak of innocence.

Thomas Cruise Mapother IV was born in Syracuse, New York, the third of four children. His father was an electrical engineer. His mother taught children who had dyslexia and other learning disabilities. She herself had dyslexia, as did all four of her children.

Dyslexia is a neurological condition that distorts, or confuses, the way printed words appear on the page. To a person with dyslexia, letters may seem to be backward or jumbled. Sometimes the white background of the page stands out, making the black letters difficult to read. Tom Cruise recalls that when he was in kindergarten, he couldn't tell "whether letters like C or D curved to the right or to the left."

At home, Tom was a bright, lively boy who imitated television characters and loved to put on skits. But at school he felt like a failure. His family moved often, and he constantly was faced with new teachers and classmates who didn't understand his problem. Altogether he attended eight different grade schools and three high schools. Because of his dyslexia, Tom often was placed in special remedial-reading classes. Though he desperately needed extra help, the special classes made him feel singled out and isolated from his peers.

When Tom was eleven, his parents were divorced. With his mother and three sisters, he moved to Louisville, Kentucky, where his mom tried to keep the family above water by taking one low-paying job after another. One year money was so short that she couldn't afford to buy Christmas presents. She and the children wrote poems for each other and shared them as gifts on Christmas morning.

The divorce and his family's poverty left Tom feeling more vulnerable than ever. His sisters shared his fear and uncertainty, as well as his constant struggle with the printed word. One day, as the four children walked to school, Tom declared, "Let's just get through this. If we can just get through this somehow!"

Tom soon discovered that he could "get through it" with the help of sports. He flung himself into hockey, wrestling, baseball, lacrosse, and skiing. Through his involvement in organized athletics, he made new friends and gained confidence.

When Tom was sixteen, his mother remarried, and the family moved to Glen Ridge, New Jersey. One day Tom was injured during wrestling practice. Since he had to limit his athletic activities for a while, he decided to audition for the school play, the musical *Guys and Dolls*. He won the lead role in the play and discovered that he felt at home and relaxed onstage. At last, he had truly found a way to express himself. In a glow of excitement after the opening performance, he asked his mother and stepfather to give him ten years to make it in show business.

After graduating from high school, Tom went to New York City, a hub of activity for hopeful young actors. Sharing an apartment with a friend, Tom worked as a restaurant busboy and attended as many acting auditions as he could. Within months, he got his lucky break. He landed a supporting role in the movie *Endless Love*, a teenage love story. One Hollywood insider recalled of Tom, "He was very

New Jersey, less polished than he is now. He was like a greaser. He had big muscles, he had hair greased back, he had an angry edge to him."

Once he broke into the movies, other roles followed in quick succession. In *Taps*, Tom Cruise (the screen name he had adopted) played a teenager who leads a bloody uprising at a military academy. Later he took a small role in *The Outsiders*, a movie based on the classic S. E. Hinton novel about troubled youths in Tulsa, Oklahoma. For both of these films, Cruise drew on the frustration of his own childhood to portray explosively angry young men. In order to play such a role, he felt that he had to understand the character's fears. It was fear, he explained, that drove these men to fight. The role that made him a top-billed star was in *Risky Business*, about a high-school boy who gets into serious (but comedic) trouble when his parents go out of town for a weekend.

With each of his roles, Tom Cruise works hard to portray his characters physically, as well as psychologically. He might gain or lose as much as 15 pounds (16.8 kg) in order to look the part of a character he is depicting. Once he had a gold cap removed from a tooth to give himself the proper jagged-tooth grin. To prepare for his role in *Top Gun*, a movie about navy flight school, he spent weeks with navy pilots, studying their speech and body language. His performance won him wide acclaim. According to one critic, "Of all the teen idols, Cruise is the most sophisticated, the most appealing, the most capable of tackling a wide dramatic range—an actor, not a talking poster."

As he matured into adulthood, Tom Cruise branched into more diverse roles. He played to high acclaim in such movies as *Rainman* and *A Few Good Men*, and for his portrayal of a paraplegic Vietnam veteran in *Born on the Fourth of July*, Cruise was nominated for an Academy Award. In 1996, he became a full-scale Hollywood force when he not only starred in, but also produced the blockbuster hit *Mission:Impossible*. In Hollywood, Tom Cruise is known as a tireless worker who is always willing to give of his time for a good cause. "His road was never paved," remarked producer Don Simpson. "It was always full of potholes, and he jumped over all of them."

JACKIE JOYNER-KERSEE

1962–

Olympic Athlete

Crime and despair stalked the streets of East St. Louis, Illinois, one of the most impoverished cities in the United States. But when Jaqueline Joyner was born, her grandmother insisted that she be named after Jaqueline Kennedy, America's glamorous First Lady. "Some day," her grandmother said, "this girl will be the first lady of something."

Jackie Joyner began life with many strikes against her. Her parents were still in their teens—her father was nineteen, her mother only seventeen. Jackie once described her house as "nothing but wallpaper over cardboard." When she was eleven, she saw a man shot in front of her house. Jackie's mother worked as a nurse's aide, and her father was a railway switchman in Springfield, Illinois, two hours away. Despite their poverty, the Joyners set high goals for their four children.

When she was nine years old, Jackie entered her first track-and-field competition at the Mayor Brown Center, an East St. Louis youth center. In her first race, Jackie finished last. Instead of feeling discouraged, however, she took her defeat as a challenge. She entered again, and this time her performance was better.

At first, Jackie's parents discouraged her interest in track and field, which they believed was an inappropriate activity for a girl. Then one day Jackie came home jubilant and announced, "I got first place, Daddy!" After that, her parents recognized that track could give her an invaluable sense of confidence, a chance to excel at something she truly enjoyed.

By the time she was twelve, Jackie showed a remarkable talent in the long jump. In one meet, she jumped 17 feet. Her coach at the Mayor Brown Center began talking to her about the Olympics. The best way to qualify for the U.S. Olympic Team was to train for a variety of events. Jackie practiced such track-and-field events as long jump, javelin throw, and the 100-meter and 800-meter races. She also played volleyball and basketball in high school, but the long jump remained her finest achievement. During her junior year, she set a state record of 20 feet, $7\frac{1}{2}$ inches. By the time she graduated, she was acclaimed as the finest woman athlete in Illinois.

Jackie Joyner graduated from high school in the top 10 percent of her class. In the fall, she enrolled in the University of California at Los Angeles (UCLA), where she had won a basketball scholarship. She was thrilled to be entering college and living in an exciting new city that was far from home. But Jackie's happiness was shattered in her freshman year, when her mother died suddenly of meningitis at the age of thirty-eight. For months, Jackie struggled to keep up with her studies and athletic training, though she felt mired in grief. As time passed, however, she found that her loss gave her "a clearer sense of reality."

At UCLA, Jackie began working with assistant track coach Bob Kersee. She was concentrating on basketball, and her track-and-field skills were not being put to use. Kersee was dazzled by Jackie's untapped talent, which he felt was going to waste. He went to the head of the athletics department and asked to work with Jackie directly. He became Jackie's coach, a relationship that sustained her throughout her career.

Kersee encouraged Jackie to take up the heptathlon, a grueling combination of seven track-and-field events. The standard heptathlon consists of the 200-meter dash, 100-meter hurdle race, high jump, long jump, shot put, javelin throw, and 800-meter run. It demands extraordinary discipline and stamina. Jackie plunged into the training with gusto. "I like the heptathlon," she explained later, "because it shows you what you're made of."

Sometimes during workouts and races, Jackie felt short of breath and wheezed uncontrollably. For five years, she had tried to ignore her condition, pushing herself even when she could hardly breathe. Finally one of her teammates persuaded her to see a doctor. In 1983, Jackie learned that she had EIA, or exercise-induced asthma. She also discovered that she was allergic to molds, dog hair, pollen, feathers, fish, nuts, and eggs. To control her asthma, doctors prescribed daily medication and inhalers. They also recommended some changes in her workout routines, which could keep her illness under control. For example, on smoggy days she should practice on an indoor track. The doctors emphasized that she must learn "to work with the condition, not against it."

At first, Jackie tried to deny that she had a problem. She was used to being in complete control of her body, and she felt now that it had betrayed her. But she soon learned that she felt better when she made a few compromises with her asthma. She no longer ignored her condition; she found ways to work with it.

Asthma never interfered with Jackie Joyner's athletic performance. In fact, her only major physical setback was unrelated to asthma. She needed a full year to recover from a 1983 hamstring pull. But by 1984, Jackie was back on the world's athlete stage. Both Jackie and her older brother, Al, became members of the U.S. Olympic track-and-field team. But once she began competing in the heptathlon, Jackie's dream was on the brink of disaster. She did poorly in the long jump, which was usually her strongest event. During the 800-meter run, she found herself falling behind the field. Suddenly she heard a familiar voice beside her, shouting, "Pump your arms! This is it!" Her brother Al had taken time out from his own triple-jump event to run alongside. Inspired by his loyalty, Jackie surged ahead and captured a second-place silver medal.

Over the years, a deep emotional bond had formed between Jackie and her coach. In 1986, they were married, and Jackie linked their names together, becoming Jackie Joyner-Kersee. Two years later, her name became one for the record books. At the 1988 Olympics in Seoul, South Korea, Joyner-Kersee was the most dominant woman in the track-and-field competition. She set a world heptathlon record and captured two gold medals in all. Sportswriters began referring to Jackie as the greatest living athlete in the United States. She repeated as heptathlon champion at the 1992 Summer Olympics and won a bronze medal in long jump at the 1996 Olympics.

Jackie Joyner-Kersee continues to test her limits, to break her own records and those of others. She is keenly aware that she is a role model for young people, especially for African-American girls from the inner city. "I remember where I came from, and I keep that in mind," she says. "If young females see the environment I grew up in and see my dreams and goals come true, they will realize their dreams and goals may also come true."

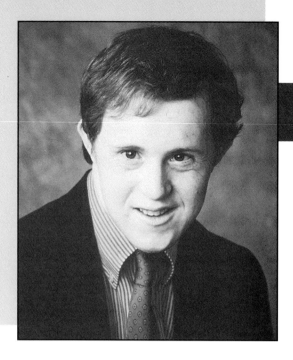

CHRIS BURKE

∽

1965–

Actor

At the age of five, Chris Burke had a small part in a school play, *The Emperor's New Clothes.* He had two lines: "Hark! Who goes there?" and "Ha ha ha! What a joke!" Although his part was small, Chris loved being on stage, and he thrilled to the sound of applause. At home that night, he told his mother that he wanted to be an actor when he grew up. But his mother shook her head sadly. Acting was a difficult field to break into, she explained. Besides, she knew that very few parts existed for someone like Chris, who had Down syndrome. A career in the theater seemed beyond his reach.

Soon after Chris was born, nurses noticed a slightly Asian tilt to his eyes. Within hours, a doctor informed his parents that the baby was a "Mongoloid." He would never learn to walk or talk, would never lead a satisfying life. The Burkes were told to place him in an institution and try to forget him.

The Burkes were devastated by the news, but they never considered abandoning their son. Though his future looked bleak, they took him home and welcomed him into the family. Chris's two teenage sisters and his twelve-year-old brother cuddled him and played with him. They wheeled his stroller up and down the streets of New York, talking to him about everything they saw. Chris was such a happy, responsive baby, it was hard to believe the doctors' grim predictions.

Chris's parents soon learned that "Mongolism" was the outmoded name for a condition called Down syndrome. Most people have twenty-three pairs of chromosomes, rodlike structures within each cell that carry genetic information. People with Down syndrome have an extra chromosome, giving them a total of forty-seven. This condition might cause them to have heart problems, poor coordination, speech difficulties, and mild to severe mental retardation. People with this condition have an extra crease in their eyelids, causing their eyes to look slightly Asian. This trait gave rise to the term "Mongolism" in the late nineteenth century.

As a preschooler, Chris Burke attended the Kennedy Child Study Center, a special program for children with mental retardation. Already he had proved the doctors wrong. Not only could he walk and talk, he was keenly interested in other people and was unusually sensitive to their needs. He always was ready to help his classmates and to comfort anyone who seemed worried or sad. Best of all, he loved to perform. He delighted the other children by singing TV commercials or imitating characters from *Sesame Street*. It was hard to understand his words, but his spirit was unmistakable.

When he was eight, Chris completed the program at the Kennedy Center. His parents visited special classes at several public schools but felt that the children were not really being challenged. Then they discovered the Cardinal Cushing School, a boarding school in Hanover, Massachusetts. The teachers at the Cushing School believed that all children had the ability to learn, even those who had been labeled mentally retarded. Though it hurt them to send their son so far away, Chris's parents decided that the Cardinal Cushing School offered him the best possible opportunity for a good education.

Chris attended the Cushing School until he was thirteen. Then he transferred to a residential school near Philadelphia that also was designed for students with retardation. Most weekends he went home, taking the train to New

York by himself. Though he spent much of the year at boarding school, he remained very close to his family. The love of his parents and siblings gave him a deep sense of confidence in himself. He understood that he had a disability and that some things were hard for him to learn. But he rarely felt ashamed or inferior to others. Once when he saw a UPS truck on the street, Chris told his father, "That's what I have, Up syndrome." After that, he referred to his condition in this way "because I feel happy and excited about my life."

Chris was a gentle boy who loved to meet new people. But outside of school, people were not always happy to deal with him. On a field trip, Chris and his classmates were told to sit in a separate waiting room, where no one else would have to see them. Sometimes other teenagers teased cruelly. A boy once stuffed pine needles into Chris's mouth. Some of the needles lodged in his lung, and he had to have a serious operation to remove them.

As he grew up, Chris never lost his passion for acting. At a summer camp for teens with disabilities, he wrote skits and put them on for the campers and their families. At home, he spent endless hours watching movies, memorizing lines, and learning about his favorite stars. He was fascinated by the series *Little House on the Prairie*, in which one of the main characters was blind. It was the only time he had seen a person with a disability as a regular character in a television series. Chris's family worried that his ambitions were unrealistic, and they discouraged him from talking about Hollywood. But Chris insisted that he would be a star.

One day in 1985 Chris called his parents from school in wild excitement. A television drama called *The Fall Guy* had a special guest star—a ten-year-old boy named Jason Kingsley, who had Down syndrome. This was the first time in his life that Chris had seen anyone with Down syndrome in a role on television. He wrote to Jason's mother, Emily Kingsley, explaining that he, too, had Down syndrome, and that he wanted to be an actor. The Kingsleys invited the Burkes to a picnic at their home in the New York suburbs. Emily Kingsley later recalled: "It was a rare opportunity to get to know someone a little older than

Jason, to get insights into his future. We didn't have many people to look to for a really clear view of what the future was going to be. . . . When I saw Chris, I saw that a young adult with Down syndrome could be this attractive, this capable, this smart, with such a great sense of humor. He was the fulfillment of all our dreams."

Encouraged by Jason Kingsley's success, Chris enrolled in a theater class for disabled students, held near his school in Pennsylvania. He attended the class for two years, learning about improvisation, costumes, and set design. His work in theater also improved his speech and his reading skills.

After graduating from school at the age of twenty-one, Chris began to search for work. He applied for jobs as a messenger or a supermarket stockboy, but again and again he was turned away. At last, deeply discouraged, he took a job in a sheltered workshop for people with disabilities. All day he sat in a big, echoing room, doing boring work on an assembly line. The supervisor insisted on absolute silence. "I hated it," Chris said later. "They wouldn't let me talk or do anything. I said, 'I'll never go back to a workshop again.'" When his mother stopped by to visit, she was appalled. Chris looked blank and lifeless. For the first time, she saw him "acting retarded." She took him home, and he never went back.

Since a paid job seemed out of reach, Chris began volunteer work at P. S. 138, a public school near his home. He worked in a special education classroom with children who had multiple disabilities. He loved the children, and they responded to his warmth and eagerness to help. His family hoped that the experience might lead to a paying job.

Then one day, the Burkes received a call from Emily Kingsley. A Hollywood director, Michael Braverman, was seeking a young actor with Down syndrome for a role in a TV pilot. Would Chris like to try out for the part? Chris was ecstatic. Perhaps his lifelong dream was about to come true! Braverman was deeply impressed when he saw the videos of Chris's audition and knew immediately that Chris was right for the part. Chris still had to audition for Warner Brothers and ABC, but he came through with flying colors.

The experience of filming was even more fascinating than Chris had imagined. "Everything surprised me," he said later, "the sets, the cameras, the way they make everything look, the way they do the lighting." Chris's father helped him learn his lines. Meg Foster, who played his mother on the show, concluded, "[Chris] is a remarkable human being, extraordinarily passionate and talented. There is a joy and love of life and being in the moment which is an actor's goal. Chris doesn't have to work for that. He is the moment. He is the actor."

The pilot program, "Desperate," aired on ABC in September 1987. But the show did not become a series. After the excitement died down, life settled back to normal. Chris was hired by P.S. 138 to operate the school's elevator. It was the first time the school district ever had employed a person with mental retardation. Chris got to know everyone in the building and made friends with some of the teachers and aides. But his experience with "Desperate" had heightened his interest in acting. He obtained an agent, but she had no luck finding him another role. Hollywood just wasn't creating many roles for people with disabilities of any kind.

As Chris rode from floor to floor at P.S. 138, Michael Braverman was in Hollywood, designing a new television series. He was so impressed by Chris Burke's ability on screen that he wanted to give him the starring role. The series, *Life Goes On*, depicted the Thatchers, a working-class family in which the middle child, Corky, has Down syndrome. It was a revolutionary idea. Never before had a family series featured a child with a disability as a central character.

In May 1989, Chris Burke and his father went back to Hollywood to film the first thirteen episodes of *Life Goes On*. The work was hard, and sometimes Chris grew frustrated. There was so much happening on the set that he would get distracted and make mistakes. If other actors grew impatient with him, he felt tense and unhappy, but he was seldom discouraged for long. He was doing what he always had longed to do, and he loved it.

ABC premiered *Life Goes On* on September 12, 1989. The show was well received by the public, and it drew an audience of about fourteen million people every week. The program ran until the spring of 1993.

The scriptwriters for *Life Goes On* tried to deal realistically with the subject of Down syndrome. They met often with teenagers who had Down syndrome and drew many plot ideas from the experiences these young people described. The program demonstrated to millions of people that Down syndrome need not be a tragedy, that life did indeed go on from there.

The television series made Chris Burke a celebrity. He toured the country, appearing on talk shows and speaking before civic groups. At restaurants and shopping malls, people crowded around him, asking for his autograph. In 1990, the Burkes were invited to the White House, where Chris made a public service announcement about Down syndrome with President George Bush. "We have gone from the depths of despair when Chris was born to the heights of unbelievable experiences like this," Chris's mother exclaimed. "Chris has opened doors for us that we would never have gone through. We know we would never have gotten up to those doors, never mind walked through them. Chris takes it all in stride. We're the ones in awe."

After *Life Goes On* was canceled, Chris Burke appeared in several made-for-TV movies and series episodes. He also recorded two albums of songs with his friends, Joe and John de Masi. Today he is employed as "goodwill ambassador" by the National Down Syndrome Society in New York City. In his job, he gives frequent talks and edits a quarterly newsletter called *News and Views*.

Chris Burke uses every opportunity to explain that people who have Down syndrome want to be treated like everyone else. Regarding his own career, he says, "I want to work hard at being an actor, and that is what is important to me. . . . Maybe someday they'll just describe me as Chris Burke, the actor."

Disabled Students in the Mainstream

On a September morning in 1989, six-year-old Ian Drummond stepped into a first-grade classroom in Woodland Park, Colorado. The other first-graders studied him curiously. The day before, their teacher and Ian's mother had explained that Ian would be joining them. The students had watched a video of Ian sliding down slides and splashing in a pool like any other six-year-old. But, Ian's mother explained, Ian had a condition called autism. In some ways, he was different from most kids his age. For one thing, he did not speak; he pressed buttons on a computer that talked for him. Loud noises made him scream with pain, and he grew frightened if he could not follow a strict routine. Still, Ian's mother had said that he was a pretty cool kid, and the teacher agreed.

At first, Ian spent only a short time in the regular first-grade classroom. He came in for math, story time, recess, and lunch hour. For the rest of the school day, he was in a "resource room." A resource room is a classroom where chil-

Many education experts believe that "special-education" classes are harmful because they are less challenging than classes that include both disabled and nondisabled students.

dren with special needs can receive extra help. As the months passed, Ian spent more and more time with the regular class. An aide was on hand to give him any extra help he needed, or to take him out for quiet time if he became upset. Ian loved school, and he worked hard to be like the other first-graders. His fellow students learned from him, too. They began to understand that outward differences were less important than they had ever imagined.

Until the mid-1970s, children with autism or other severe disabilities had almost no chance to attend regular schools. Most were enrolled in special classes reserved for children with disabilities. Some lived away from home during the school year at residential schools for the deaf, blind, or emotionally disturbed. According to a report issued in 1973, some 750,000 disabled children were not in school at all.

In the early 1950s, New Jersey began to place blind students in regular public-school classes. The students had Braille copies of the textbooks that their classmates were using, and they typed out their assignments in print for their teachers to read. For most blind children, this arrangement worked very well. Parents and students generally preferred this form of "integrated education" over the old system of special classes.

Throughout most of the country, however, educators clung to the notion that children with disabilities belonged in separate programs. Teachers claimed that only a specially equipped classroom and a specially trained staff could meet the disabled child's needs. They warned that a child who was blind or who used a wheelchair might be teased by nondisabled classmates and would be happier "with others like himself."

In general, special-education classes were less demanding than classes for nondisabled students. Teachers seemed to believe that students with disabilities could not perform academically and rarely pushed them to do their best. Many disabled children never were challenged to study such subjects as science and geography. They were excluded from physical education and did not go on field trips.

A blind student reading a Braille picture book

To make matters worse, special-education students were socially isolated. Special classes separated them from their peers, often creating a deep sense of inferiority. Looking back on her years in a special class, one woman recalled: "The handicapped and retarded classrooms were tucked away in a corner of the school basement. Our only activity with other children was the weekly school assembly. We never participated in any school program. We watched. Although the school lunchroom was also in the basement, we ate lunch in our classrooms. . . . The only contact we had with the normal children was visual. On these occasions I can report my own feelings: envy. Given the loud, clear message that was daily being delivered to them, I feel quite confident that I can also report their feelings: yuck!"

In 1975, Congress passed Public Law 94-142, the Education for All Handicapped Children Act. (Today the law is known as the Individuals with Disabilities Education Act, or IDEA.) This law stated that all children, regardless of disability, are entitled to a free public education. It specified that children with disabilities are to be taught in "the least restrictive setting possible."

On paper, the law promised an end to segregated special education. No longer would students with disabilities be tucked away in a corner of the basement. They would learn reading, spelling, math, and social studies in neighborhood schools with nondisabled classmates. They would still have access to special training when necessary. Blind students would be taught Braille; deaf students would learn lip-reading or American Sign Language; students with learning disabilities would have one-on-one help with reading or math. But the regular class would be the disabled student's base of operations. She or he would be involved in ordinary school activities as completely as possible. The practice of teaching disabled students in regular classrooms came to be known as "mainstreaming."

Most school districts, however, have been reluctant to put mainstreaming fully into effect. Many schools still maintain special classes for students who are deaf, blind, or have orthopedic disabilities. The list of special programs that attempts to educate disabled children is as confusing as alphabet soup: CRMD (children with retarded mental development), LD (learning disabled), EMH (emotionally/mentally handicapped). Children in these special classes usually study some subjects in regular classrooms, but the resource room is their home base. They still see themselves, and are seen by others, as separate from the main student body.

By 1990, studies found that 67 percent of all students with disabilities were

"Mainstreaming" is the practice of teaching disabled students in regular classrooms.

still in resource rooms or special residential schools. These students face the same problems—isolation and low educational standards—that plagued generations of disabled students before IDEA. Mainstreamed students, too, are sometimes unhappy with their situation at school. Some are not adequately taught crucial skills, such as Braille and independent travel for blind students. Some are not allowed to take gym classes or science labs. Some feel that teachers expect less from them than from other students and give them good grades for mediocre work. As a high-school student with cerebral palsy explained, "You begin to question yourself. Are you smart, or are they making exceptions? It confuses you."

For most students, extracurricular activities play an important role in school life. Here again, disabled students often encounter problems. Stairs may keep students with wheelchairs from using some parts of the school building. Deaf students cannot take part in after-school activities if sign-language interpreters are not available. A teacher may discourage a blind student from trying out for the gymnastics team, fearing that she or he might get hurt.

Despite these obstacles, many mainstreamed students thrive academically, take part in every aspect of school life, and make lasting friends. April, a blind high-school student, reflected: "If a teacher treats me normally, that helps a lot of students. They realize I'm just a normal person. They don't have to be especially nice to me like I'm going to get offended or break or something. Clubs help a lot. Being outside of the classroom itself and in extracurricular activities is good. You get to do a lot of things, to talk about a lot of things besides what you're doing in class that day."

In the 1990s, educators began to discuss a concept known as "full inclusion." In essence, full inclusion is mainstreaming without the wrinkles. It calls for students with disabilities to be truly integrated, not only into regular classrooms, but into all school activities. It can work only if students are taught all the skills they need and are provided with any necessary adaptive equipment. All school programs, in and out of the classroom, must be made barrier-free. In

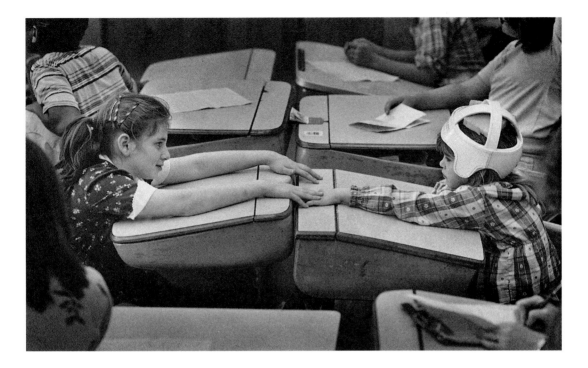

such an environment, students who are disabled can truly function as equals beside their nondisabled classmates.

After twenty years, some people with disabilities wonder whether IDEA has made any difference at all. "What the law is doing best today," says disability rights activist Adrienne Asch, "is giving parents, advocates, and disabled students something against which to measure what they have. Before there was nothing. . . . [The law] should be understood to require equal access to all of the school's life for all the students who are in it."

MARLEE MATLIN

1 9 6 5 –

Actor

W hen Marlee Matlin remembers her childhood, she says: "I fought. I never hid anything. My mother was very strong and very feisty, and that's probably where I picked it up from. I grew up thinking that I'm going to be independent, deaf or not, that no one's going to control me."

Marlee Matlin grew up in Morton Grove, Illinois, a suburb of Chicago. When she was eighteen months old, she contracted roseola, usually a mild disease of early childhood. In her case, however, the illness was severe, and it left her almost totally deaf.

Marlee's parents wanted her to have the widest possible range of options. They obtained training for her in the two major communications methods available to deaf children—lip-reading and American Sign Language (ASL). Marlee became a proficient lip-reader by the time she was five years old, but in general, she and her family found signing more efficient. ASL became Marlee's primary means of communication.

Marlee Matlin never attended a residential school for the deaf. Instead, she went to public schools that offered special programs for hearing-impaired students. She attended regular classes with sign-language interpreters who translated the teachers' spoken words. Nevertheless, she felt frustrated when she could not understand the flow of conversation around her. Occasionally classmates teased her about her deafness, throwing her into wild temper tantrums. "I wanted to be perfect, and I couldn't accept my deafness," she recalled years later. "I was so angry and frightened."

When she was eight years old, Marlee Matlin began to perform with a children's theater group at the Center for Deafness in Des Plaines, Illinois. From the beginning, she displayed remarkable talent for acting. In her first major role, she played Dorothy in a production of *The Wizard of Oz*. She remained active with the group for seven years, performing throughout the Midwest in such plays as *Mary Poppins* and *Peter Pan*.

By the time she entered high school, however, Marlee was growing tired of the theater. "I had a boyfriend, I had a car, I had everything a high-school student wanted," she explained. "I didn't need to act." For the next few years, she pursued other interests, convinced that her acting days were behind her. When she enrolled in Harper College at Palatine, Illinois, she planned to major in criminal justice. She hoped to become a police officer. She soon realized that her deafness would be an obstacle in most branches of police work, and that she probably would be confined to a desk job. Discouraged, she dropped out of college.

Just before she left Harper, Marlee Matlin learned that auditions were being held for a Chicago production of the play *Children of a Lesser God*. The drama, which had won wide acclaim on Broadway, is the story of a deaf woman and her relationship with a hearing man. Playwright Mark Medoff required that in every production all the deaf characters must be played by deaf actors. Marlee Matlin went to the tryouts and was awarded the role of Lydia, one of the play's minor characters. During the show's run in Chicago, Paramount Pictures began work on a film version of the story. An international search was conducted for a deaf actress who could take the leading role of Sarah Norman, an intensely angry young woman determined that the world must accept her on her own terms. The director studied videos of every actress who had played Sarah in stage productions, rejecting one after another. But in the video of the current Chicago production, the director saw a brief scene of Marlee Matlin playing Lydia and was immediately impressed. Paramount flew Matlin to New York for an audition, and then to Los Angeles for further readings. In the end, she was awarded the role.

Children of a Lesser God was a major film event in more ways than one. Not only was it a big hit, it also was the first Hollywood movie in which deaf actors were hired to portray deaf characters. Paramount hired interpreters for Matlin and the nine other hearing-impaired actors involved in the production. A hearing-impaired technical advisor also worked with the film crew. Yet overall, *Children of a Lesser God* is a movie not about deafness but about the complexity of human relationships. "It's about talking and listening," Marlee Matlin explained in an interview. "It's about deaf people, and it's about love, and it's about communication. It's about rejection, about giving and taking, about patience."

When *Children of a Lesser God* premiered in October 1986, critics were virtually unanimous in their praise of Marlee Matlin's performance. *Time* magazine called her "an actress of awesome gifts." *Newsweek* claimed she was "so good, sensitive, sharp, funny, that she's likely to be the first deaf actress to get an Oscar nomination." *Newsweek* was on the money. Not only was Matlin nominated for an Oscar, she won the Academy Award for Best Actress in March 1987. She was the first deaf actress to be so highly honored, and at age twenty-one, she was the youngest actress to win this award.

Despite her success, however, Marlee Matlin found it difficult to build her acting career. She discovered that there were very few movie or television productions with leading deaf characters. Those that did exist were often poorly written or overly sentimental. In December 1987, Matlin appeared in her second feature film, *Walker*. The movie was a box-office flop and a critical disaster. Later she explained that she only accepted the role of a hearing-impaired

Marlee Matlin made a strong statement when she addressed a television audience using sign language.

woman who dies early in the film because she feared that nothing else might come her way for a long time.

At the 1988 Academy Awards ceremony, Marlee Matlin was chosen to present the award for Best Actor. She began her presentation in ASL with her words spoken by an interpreter who stood off camera. Then, to the amazement of her hearing audience, she stopped signing and spoke her words aloud. For several months, she had been taking intensive speech therapy, and her speech was now clearer than ever before.

While hearing audiences applauded Matlin's accomplishment, many members of the deaf community were dismayed. By choosing to deliver her address in spoken English, did Matlin suggest that speech was somehow more acceptable than sign? In a letter to the *New York Times*, Matlin tried to end the controversy: "The United States contains more than 26 million hearing-impaired individuals," she stated, "each different in his or her preference for a mode of communication. I choose which mode is best for me and which I do well. I do not sign and speak simultaneously, and when I choose to sign alone with an off-camera voice, or to speak alone, as I did on the Oscar ceremony telecast, I couldn't potentially ignore the two major segments of the deaf community, those who use speech and do not sign, and those who sign and do not use speech. Fortunately, the telecast was closed-captioned with subtitles for viewers who have decoding devices. Everyone, regardless of communications preference, had access."

In 1991, Marlee Matlin made a professional breakthrough. Television director Robert Singer was seeking an actress to play the role of Tess Coffman, a stubborn young lawyer in a new NBC television series called *Reasonable Doubt*. Singer had never envisioned that the character might be deaf, but when Marlee Matlin auditioned for the part, everything fell into place. The show was a hit, and Matlin won praise for her work.

Marlee Matlin uses her high profile to serve as a spokesperson for deaf and hearing-impaired people throughout the country. She is a strong advocate for closed-captioning, a system by which speech in television programs is presented as onscreen text for viewers with a special decoding device. Matlin refuses to appear in any film or television show that is not captioned. Her work has helped to make the television industry more aware that deaf viewers are a large and valuable audience.

Marlee Matlin always has seen herself not as a deaf actress, but as an actress who happens to be deaf. "Her whole body is in constant motion, almost dancing as she is standing still," a reporter wrote in *Parade* magazine. "Her face is extremely expressive, a trait in many deaf people who have learned to communicate visually, and a real boon for an actress." Matlin's first concern is to develop her talent, to explore her potential through challenging new roles, to become the best that she can be in her chosen profession."

∽

1966–

Athlete

When Jean Driscoll was born in Milwaukee, Wisconsin, doctors told her parents that she would never walk, never go to school, never have a meaningful life. Jean was born with spina bifida, a condition in which the spinal cord is not completely formed. The spinal cord is a complex set of nerves running through the spinal column, or backbone, and connecting to every part of the body. People with spina bifida may be partially paralyzed and often have trouble with bladder or bowel control.

To the amazement of the doctors, Jean began to walk when she was two years old, wearing leg braces to support her ankles. She also proved the doctors wrong when she entered kindergarten like any other child. By the time she was in second grade, she had learned to ride a bicycle. She was painfully aware that most people didn't expect her to amount to much. Even as a small child, she was determined to show them that they were wrong.

Despite her best efforts, however, Jean could not hide the fact that she had a disability. She often felt awkward and clumsy because of the braces on her legs. Worse still, she wore diapers at night until fifth grade because of her bowel and bladder problems. Her parents never fully explained her medical condition to her brothers and sisters. Sometimes they teased her, calling her cruel names.

One day when she was in the ninth grade, Jean made a fast turn on her bike, lost her balance, and fell. For most people, it would have been a minor accident. But years of walking had strained Jean's leg and hip muscles. The fall dislocated her hip, and she spent the next year in and out of the hospital. She underwent five operations and lived for months in a body cast, only to be told that her hip never would heal properly. She would have to start using a wheelchair.

When she returned to school, Jean was hopelessly behind in her studies. Before the accident, she had been an honor student enrolled in a challenging preparatory school. Now she had to transfer to a public school, away from all her old friends. Teachers told her she should take a secretarial course. After all, she had to spend most of her time sitting down—why not do it in front of a computer screen?

Using crutches, Jean still was able to walk short distances, but if she had to cover much ground, she used a wheelchair. She felt very isolated, set apart from the nondisabled people around her. When she thought about the future, she was discouraged and frightened.

One other student with spina bifida, a boy who also used a wheelchair, was enrolled at Jean's school. He played on a wheelchair soccer team and suggested that Jean should come to one of their games. Jean wanted no part of wheelchair sports. She imagined a bunch of frail, sickly people gingerly rolling around on a field and pretending to have a good time. Wheelchair sports sounded very second-rate—not even close to "real" athletics.

But the boy at school didn't give up on her. She agreed to attend one of his practices, hoping that he would finally leave her in peace. To her amazement, Jean was swept up in the excitement of the game. The players zoomed up and down the field, spinning and dodging. Sometimes they collided and tumbled from their wheelchairs, only to scramble back and go on playing. "It was rough, it was down and dirty!" she remembers. "There was nothing second-rate about it!"

Jean Driscoll
238

Wheelchair sports opened a whole new world for Jean. She threw herself into wheelchair soccer and tried other wheelchair sports, such as hockey, softball, and football. She was delighted whenever her friend Kathy, who was not disabled, came to watch her games. Even as a spectator in the stands, Kathy found wheelchair sports exciting.

Soon after high school, Jean entered her first wheelchair road race. She used a makeshift racing chair built from plumber's plastic piping. By the end of the 5-mile (8-km) course, she was exhausted. Her hands were raw and blistered from turning the wheels. She decided that racing was not for her.

Not long afterward, however, Jean watched a national championship wheelchair track meet. She was impressed by the grace and stamina of the athletes, and she decided to try racing again. But she needed a lightweight racing wheelchair, which would cost her about two thousand dollars.

Milwaukee's wheelchair sports program was organized by the Division of Recreation within the public schools, together with the local center for independent living. The people who ran the program sought sponsors for some of its leading athletes. Jim Derse, a Milwaukee businessman with a deep commitment to young people with disabilities, became Jean Driscoll's sponsor. He bought her the racing wheelchair she needed and remained her loyal supporter as her athletic career unfolded.

After graduating from high school, Jean enrolled in a nursing program at the University of Wisconsin in Milwaukee. She had become very close with some of the nurses who cared for her when she had dislocated her hip, and they were important role models in her life. She remained passionately involved with sports, but deep down she was very unhappy with herself. When she wasn't on the playing field, she resisted using a wheelchair. She forced herself to walk with crutches, no matter how tiring or painful it was for her. She still was fighting the image of herself as a person with a disability. To make the situation even worse, her parents were getting divorced. Jean's grades slumped, and after three semesters she was forced to drop out of college.

Jean Driscoll in action

This period was one of the worst in Jean's life. She felt hopeless, a total failure. Fortunately, a nurse she had known in the hospital offered her a job as a live-in baby-sitter. Jean always had loved children, and she needed to earn money and to live away from home. The job was just the right thing at the right time.

During the year she worked as a mother's helper, Jean attended a wheelchair sports workshop in Milwaukee. There she met an athletics recruiter from the University of Illinois at Urbana. Illinois had an extensive wheelchair sports program. The school searched for promising wheelchair athletes, just as it tried to lure nondisabled athletes for its other teams. Jean entered the University of Illinois in 1987 and eventually earned a B.A. in speech communications and an M.S. in rehabilitation administration. She studied hard, but the athletics program truly shaped her life. She took part in both basketball and racing. Her coach encouraged her to train for marathons, races that extend over a 26-mile (42-km) course. Many big-time marathons had begun to include men's and women's wheelchair events as legitimate categories. Jean entered the Chicago Marathon in 1989 and placed high enough to qualify for the world-famous Boston Marathon the following year.

On a clear April day in 1990, Jean Driscoll sat at the starting line in Boston. For months she had prepared for this moment, training on the flat prairies of central Illinois. But her training partner had usually come out ahead of her. She did not expect to do well in this race.

At the time, Jean did not realize that she had a distinct advantage on the hilly course in Boston. "I'm very strong," she explains. "Other people can beat me in flat country, but I pull ahead of the pack going uphill, where it takes sheer muscle." To her joy and astonishment, she placed first in the women's wheelchair category, breaking a world record. She took home $2,500 and the coveted gold medal.

For six years, beginning in 1990, Jean Driscoll has entered the Boston Marathon. She has won each year and has broken world records several times. She is the first person ever to win the Boston Marathon six consecutive times.

In addition to her success in the Boston Marathon, Jean Driscoll won a silver medal at the 1992 Olympic Games in Barcelona, Spain, which sponsored an exhibition event for wheelchair racers. Her remarkable achievements have helped bring wider recognition for wheelchair sports everywhere. She has won many awards and has even gone jogging with President Bill Clinton, who by tradition jogs with the Boston Marathon winners each year. In 1991, she received an award from the Women's Sports Foundation, which was established by tennis champion Billie Jean King and other leading female athletes to promote women's participation in sports. The award showed the world that a wheelchair racer could be a legitimate, elite athlete. "Basically, wheelchair sports are following the same path that women's sports took ten or twenty years ago," Jean remarks. "It used to be that stories about disabled athletes only turned up in the human interest pages. Now we're getting onto the sports pages where we belong."

JIM ABBOTT

1967–

Baseball Pitcher

As a boy, Jim Abbott often dreamed of becoming a pitcher for a major-league baseball team. His parents, Mike and Kathy Abbott, encouraged him. The Abbotts taught their son that he could accomplish anything if he was determined and worked hard. Jim, who is now a star pitcher in the big leagues, believes this attitude has been the secret of his success. His parents, he says, never seemed to recall that he had been born "disabled."

James Anthony Abbott was born in Flint, Michigan, on September 19, 1967. His parents were saddened to learn that their first child had been born without a right hand, but they were determined to treat Jim's disability as a challenge, rather than a handicap. When he was young, he was fitted with a prosthetic hand, but he thought it looked like a claw. Other kids called him mean names such as "Captain Hook" and "Crab." Jim soon decided to stop wearing the prosthesis.

From the beginning, Jim's parents encouraged him to do everything other children did. Jim recalls: "My having one hand was not a big issue when I was a kid. I never gave thought to having one hand." Like other boys, Jim played ball with his father, his younger brother, Chad, and his friends. When he was

eleven, he joined a Little League team as an outfielder. When the coach needed an emergency starting pitcher, Jim volunteered. To everyone's amazement,
Jim took the mound and pitched a no-hitter. Jim became a full-time pitcher
after that, and batters who assumed that Jim was a poor fielder soon learned
they were wrong. While he pitched, Jim tucked his glove under his arm.
Immediately after releasing the ball he slipped his left hand into the glove in
one swift motion. Batters tried to bunt against Jim to take advantage of his disability, but he raced off the mound, pounced on the ball, and threw out virtually every batter.

As a pitcher for Flint Central High School, Jim maintained an impressive
record. During his senior year, Jim won 10 games, lost 3, and pitched 3 no-hit-
ters. And he was a great hitter, too, batting .427 with 7 home runs. What's
more, Jim was the starting quarterback for the Central High football team!

Jim's athletic skills began to attract attention from both college and pro
scouts. As high-school graduation neared, Jim had to choose between a baseball
contract with the Toronto Blue Jays and a baseball scholarship to the University
of Michigan, whose sports teams he had followed passionately throughout his
childhood. Jim was torn between two dreams—playing pro baseball and attending the University of Michigan. In the end, Jim elected to attend Michigan; he
would get an education first and then pursue a baseball career.

Distracted by the press coverage he was receiving, Jim faltered in the
beginning of his first season with the Michigan Wolverines baseball team. He
soon settled down, however, and compiled a record of 6–2 and was voted to the
Big Ten Playoffs All-Tournament Team—a tremendous honor for a freshman
pitcher. The following year Jim had a sparkling 11–3 record and strung together a remarkable 35 straight innings without giving up an earned run.

That summer, Jim was chosen to be a starting pitcher for Team U.S.A., the
national team that would compete in the Pan-American Games in Cuba.
Though Team U.S.A. lost in the finals, Jim's pitching helped his country's team
earn a silver medal. In one game of the tournament, Jim pitched the Americans

Jim Abbott in his proudest moment—completing his no-hitter for the New York Yankees on September 4, 1993

to a stunning upset of the Cuban national team. Even though Jim was defeating their own team, the Cuban fans gave him a standing ovation every time he took the mound. Cuban leader Fidel Castro even asked Jim for his autograph. Jim's year was capped by winning the Golden Spikes Award as the finest amateur baseball player in the United States.

Jim had become perhaps the most famous college baseball player in history, yet some major-league teams doubted that the one-handed pitcher could field effectively against major-league hitters. The California Angels, however, were not among the doubters. The Angels chose Jim Abbott in the first round of the 1988 amateur draft. Prior to starting his professional career, Jim again represented his country, this time as a member of the 1988 U.S. Olympic baseball team. One of Abbott's proudest moments was the championship game of the Olympics. Jim pitched the U.S. team to a gold-medal victory.

The biggest baseball story in April 1989 was Jim Abbott, who pitched so brilliantly in spring training that he was named to the California Angels' major-league roster. In the previous quarter-century, only ten other pitchers had skipped the minor leagues entirely and debuted on a major-league roster. Most baseball fans assumed that a pitcher with one hand would need several years of training in the minor leagues. But on opening day 1989, Jim was part of the Angels' starting rotation.

Jim's first season with the Angels was a record setter. He earned twelve wins, more than any other major-league rookie. He was also voted to Topp's All-Star Rookie team. Jim spent the next three seasons in an Angels uniform. By the 1991 season, he was widely recognized as one of the best pitchers in the league. In December 1992, Jim Abbott was shocked when California traded him to the New York Yankees. Before long, however, Jim began to feel right at home with the Yankees' competitive spirit. He was a mainstay in the Yankees' rotation for the next two seasons. The biggest thrill of his life came in 1993, when he pitched a no-hitter against the Cleveland Indians, ensuring his place in the Baseball Hall of Fame. Since 1993, Jim has also played for the Chicago White Sox before returning to the Angels in 1995.

Over the years, Jim Abbott has endured countless well-meaning but thoughtless questions about his disability. He has often been portrayed by the media as a "one-handed man who can pitch," rather than as a pitcher who happens to have only one hand. While Jim has remained courteous at all times, he sometimes grows weary of the attention. Jim says, "I don't think of myself as being handicapped—I mean, my hand has not kept me from doing anything that I wanted to do. However, it's something that's always going to be part of my story. I understand that, and I'm not going to run away from it. Ideally, though, I'd prefer to be recognized for pitching well and nothing else."

HEATHER WHITESTONE

1973–

Miss America 1995

The audience cheered and the cameras flashed. Through a mist of tears, Miss Alabama stepped forward to accept the crown of Miss America. Supporters from her home state were overjoyed; this was the first time since 1951 that Miss Alabama had won the Miss America Pageant. This Miss America was unique in another way, as well. She was the first woman with a disability ever to hold the treasured crown. Heather Whitestone, Miss America 1995, was deaf.

When Heather was eighteen months old, she had a severe form of influenza. The doctor prescribed an antibiotic that saved her life, but the drug destroyed nearly all of her hearing. At first, her mother sank into despair. "The good Lord and I had six months of a real hard time," Mrs. Whitestone recalled later. "But I believe you grow in character during hardship. Good times are the reinforcers. I am grateful the good Lord didn't give up on me. I could handle it, once the peace was gotten in my heart. It was a new challenge. I could feel sorry for myself, or see what we could get done."

Heather's mother was convinced that her daughter could live a full and rewarding life, if only she believed in herself. She set out to equip Heather with

Heather Whitestone

skills and positive experiences. If Heather had confidence in herself, opportunities would come her way.

The so-called experts told Mrs. Whitestone that her expectations were unrealistic. Doctors talked about "accepting limitations." They insisted that Heather never would read beyond the third-grade level. And of course, they warned, she would not learn to speak.

Heather's mother ignored the experts when they spoke in such negative terms. As a seventh-grade math teacher, she knew that all children have the potential to learn, given the proper training and encouragement. She worked with Heather for hours every day, teaching her to lip-read and to pronounce words she could not hear. To help her understand rhythm, she enrolled her in ballet class. Heather performed ballet by feeling the vibrations of the music and by coordinating her movements with those of the other dancers. Ballet gave her a sense of rhythm that helped in her efforts to speak clearly.

In first grade, Heather entered a regular public-school class with hearing students. In the beginning, school was difficult and painful. Sometimes the other children laughed at Heather's halting speech and teased her about her hearing aid. She could not always follow what the teacher said in class. Each year she fell farther and farther behind. At last, in fourth grade, her mother sent her to the Central Institute for the Deaf, a private boarding school in St. Louis, Missouri. There Heather received intensive instruction in lip-reading and speech and made great gains academically. After three years, she returned home and entered public school as a ninth-grader, two years ahead of her former classmates.

Although Heather was popular in high school, boys sometimes were reluctant to ask her out on dates. Because of her deafness, they felt that she was different from other girls, and they were afraid to approach her. As the senior prom drew near, Heather realized that no one planned to invite her. She took the matter into her own hands and asked a boy if he would like to go with her. When he turned red with embarrassment, she feared she had made a terrible

Heather Whitestone weeps with joy moments after being named Miss America 1995.

mistake. But he was not horrified by her suggestion, he was just shy. In the end, they had a wonderful time together.

After graduation, Heather entered Jacksonville State University in Alabama. She planned to major in accounting, but ballet remained her true passion. "When I dance, I feel like I'm in a safe world," Heather says. "I remember when I was little, the other children making fun of me. But when I danced I felt free."

When Heather Whitestone began to enter beauty pageants, ballet was the special talent she displayed before the judges. Over a period of three years, she moved up from small, local competitions to the Miss Alabama contest. At last, in September 1994, she found herself in Atlantic City, New Jersey, competing for the title of Miss America.

During the competition, the judges asked each contestant about her aim in life. Heather Whitestone replied that she wanted to help children from all backgrounds to reach their full potential. She promised to encourage children to have a positive attitude; to believe in their dreams; to face their obstacles, no matter how great; to work hard; and to build a support team. In describing this five-point program, she used the metaphor of a five-pointed star. By talking to young people about her own life and its challenges, she felt sure that she could inspire them to set high goals for themselves.

As Miss America, Heather Whitestone traveled as much as 20,000 miles (32,187 km) a month, making public appearances all over the country. She worked hard to fulfill her pledge to America's young people, speaking frequently at schools and youth groups. In most of her talks, she emphasized that "anything is possible." She talked about her own "support team," her family and God, who made everything possible for her. She also urged young people to seek a good education. Learning has been one of the most crucial keys to her own success. "If I have wisdom," she says, "no one can take advantage of me and make me feel less important."

TO FIND A WAY OR TO MAKE ONE: TECHNOLOGICAL AIDS FOR THE DISABLED

When Al Mann arrived for a job interview at IBM, the personnel manager was taken aback. He had not known that the young applicant had cerebral palsy. "Why do you think you are qualified to work for our company?" he asked. "Because," Mann explained, "I'm very creative. As a person with a disability, I have learned to be flexible. There are a lot of things I can't do in the ways that nondisabled people do them. So I have to look at what needs to be done, think about all the tools I have available, and figure out my own unique method." The personnel manager was so impressed by Mann's logic that he hired him for the job.

Like Al Mann, most people with disabilities become experts at finding new ways to deal with everyday tasks. A mother with multiple sclerosis who does not have the strength to lift her infant son rolls him onto a blanket. She pulls the blanket across the carpet to move her baby from place to place. A man with memory loss from a head injury keeps extensive lists to remind him of appoint-

Simply designed wheelchairs (right) have been in use for more than a century. Today, motorized carts (left) and wheelchairs make independent travel possible for people with physical disabilities.

ments and daily chores. A blind girl feels the coldness rise on the outside of her glass as she pours her milk, and knows when the liquid is near the top. These are all simple, common-sense solutions to problems. They depend upon such ordinary household items as a blanket or a notepad, combined with an individual's abilities and interest in completing a task.

Often the disabled person's options are enhanced by using equipment designed to meet his or her special needs. This specialized equipment can be thoroughly "low-tech." No one knows who first thought of attaching wheels to a chair, giving freedom of movement to a person who could not walk. Today wheelchairs come in endless variety, including sleek sporting models in radiant colors. The long white cane, which most blind people use in independent travel, is another example of a low-tech aid. The cane acts as an extension of the user's arm, enabling him or her to feel steps and other obstacles in the path ahead. Clothing with velcro fastenings (instead of buttons) is designed for people with limited use of their hands. People with coordination problems may use spoons and forks with thick handles that can be grasped easily.

In today's world, technology has progressed beyond the wildest fantasies of past generations. People with disabilities are reaping some of the benefits of our technological revolution. Optical scanners can "read" the printed page aloud for people who are blind. People with quadriplegia zoom along city streets in motorized wheelchairs. Teletyping devices (TTYs) permit deaf people to make

The Telecommunications Device for the Deaf (TTY) converts voices on a telephone into visible text that a deaf person can read; he or she can then type responses on the keyboard.

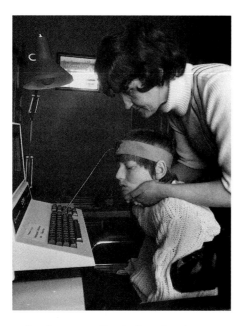

*Christopher Nolan
(seen here at age fifteen)
writes on his computer
with his mother's help.*

telephone calls. The deaf person types a message on the TTY, and it is transmitted over the telephone wires to a relay station. The relay operator reads the message aloud to the party the deaf person is calling and sends the answer back to the deaf person by TTY.

In 1989, twenty-one-year-old Christopher Nolan won Britain's prestigious Whitbread Prize for Literature with his autobiography, *Under the Eye of the Clock*. Nolan, who has cerebral palsy, cannot speak or move his hands or feet. He wrote his book by using a computer, which he operates with movements of his head. Computers have opened the channels of communication for many people like Nolan, who cannot speak or write with a pen. Some computers pronounce words aloud when the user types them on a keyboard. For people whose movements are more limited, there are other options. Computers have even been programmed to respond to a person's eye movements. The user gazes at a letter or picture, and the machine says the name of the item out loud.

Advanced technology has opened up many new employment opportunities for people with disabilities. People who are blind now work as travel agents and airline reservation clerks. By using computers that provide Braille displays or speech output, they have access to the vast reservoir of information that is now available online through computers and modems.

The growing field of biotechnology takes high-tech advances a dizzying step further. It seeks to improve the body's functioning by using machines to replace defective human organs. One of the first developments in biotechnology was the pacemaker. Installed beneath the skin of a person's chest, the pacemaker sends out electrical impulses that correct the heart's faulty rhythm. Considered revolutionary when it appeared in the 1970s, the pacemaker has helped millions of people live longer, healthier lives. The "artificial kidney," or dialysis machine, is also in wide use. The machine filters impurities from the blood of people with kidney failure.

During the 1980s doctors began experiments with "functional electrical stimulation" (FES) for people with spinal cord injuries. A computer sends electrical impulses to more than two dozen electrodes attached to muscles in the person's leg. The electrical impulses cause the muscles to contract, enabling the leg to move. These muscle contractions can be timed so precisely that the person can stand and walk.

Biotechnology may also someday aid people who are deaf or blind. Cochlear implants already have restored limited hearing to some deaf people.

A cochlear implant can allow a deaf person to hear well enough to understand voices.

The implant replaces the cochlea, a delicate organ in the inner ear. It receives the vibrations from sounds and turns them into electrical impulses that are passed on to the brain's auditory lobe. A similar concept is used in "artificial vision." Researchers are seeking ways to send images to the visual center of a blind person's brain. So far, artificial vision is still in the experimental phase and has no practical uses. But scientists predict that it may someday be as commonplace as the pacemaker.

These advances have the ring of science fiction, and they make splashy news stories. They suggest that technology will some day eradicate disability—that blindness, deafness, and paraplegia will take their place beside the blacksmith's forge and the covered wagon. Yet many people with disabilities regard biotechnology with skepticism. The cochlear implant, for example, has stirred serious controversy within the deaf community. Though the device permits deaf people to hear some sounds, it does not restore normal hearing. In fact, many people who have the implants claim that the sounds they hear are annoying and hard to decipher. Deaf adults fear that children with cochlear implants will not wish to learn American Sign Language and other skills that would help them function as deaf persons. At the same time, they will not hear well enough to manage in the hearing world. Heralded by the media as a miracle of science, the cochlear implant may create more problems than it solves.

By the same token, many blind people express concerns about artificial vision, which does not yet come close to actual eyesight. It does not begin to eliminate the need for Braille and other skills that blind people learn in order to live independently. Yet the dream of seeing again may keep some people from learning to deal with their blindness. Wheelchair users have similar reservations about FES. FES may allow a person with paraplegia to take a few halting steps, but she or he can still move far more easily by using a wheelchair.

Hundreds of high-tech devices for disabled people are now on the market. Some have proved more helpful than others. But nearly all of them have one thing in common—their lofty price tags. Since the market for specialized equipment is relatively small, production costs remain steep. Equipment that costs several thousand dollars is beyond the means of most disabled persons. Some manage to purchase equipment through low-interest loans. Others obtain it with the help of rehabilitation agencies. But many people with disabilities still do not have access to computers and other machines that might enhance their lives.

Many people with disabilities worry that the thrust toward expensive technology is a misuse of society's resources. They contend that money and energy would be better spent in making our communities more accessible. Instead of chasing futuristic "cures," such as artificial vision, we should concentrate on the needs of disabled people today. Sometimes the problem of getting a task done can be solved with simple, low-tech, common sense.

Modern technology can help people with disabilities move more freely. It can give them greater access to information and enable them to communicate more easily with others. As engineers, programmers, and informed consumers, disabled people are working with corporations large and small to develop new products. They are trying to ensure that technology will be empowering, that it will give people with disabilities greater opportunities to fulfill their goals.

This Open Book reading machine scans books, magazines, and other printed material and converts the text into synthesized speech so that people with visual impairments can read anything.

GLOSSARY

activist
a person who uses political means to fight for a cause

American Sign Language (ASL)
a language based on signs formed with the hands, used by deaf people in the United States

Americans with Disabilities Act
a law passed in 1990 that grants civil rights protection to people with disabilities

amputee
a person who has lost, or has been born without, one or more limbs (arms or legs)

amyotropic lateral sclerosis (ALS, or Lou Gehrig's disease)
a disease of the nervous system that affects activities such as walking and speech

architectural barrier
a part of a building design that blocks access to people with disabilities (such as a doorway too narrow to allow a wheelchair to pass through)

asthma
an allergic condition that causes wheezing and shortness of breath

attitudinal barrier
a belief (or an "attitude") held by many people that effectively restricts people with disabilities from equal access to society's resources

autism
a condition that causes a person to withdraw from contact with others

Braille
a writing method using small raised dots that can be read by touch by people who are blind

cancer
any of several diseases caused by the uncontrolled growth of abnormal cells in the body

cataract
a cloudy membrane over the eye that interferes with vision

catheter
a thin plastic tube used to pass fluids in or out of the body

Center for Independent Living (CIL)
program originated in Berkeley, California, based on the concept that people with disabilities should share resources and help one another

cerebral palsy
any of several conditions caused by damage to the brain; may result in stiffness and rigidity, or in uncontrollable movements

chromosome
a rodlike structure within living cells containing thousands of genes

clubfoot
a congenital malformation of one or both feet

congenital
existing at birth

convulsion
seizure; involuntary movement caused by abnormal electrical impulses in the brain

disability
any condition that limits a person's ability to work, learn, move, communicate, or carry out such daily activities as cooking, dressing, or bathing without aid

Down syndrome
a condition in which a person is born with an extra chromosome causing coordination problems, speech difficulties, and mild to severe mental retardation

dyslexia
a neurological condition that interferes with a person's ability to learn to read

epilepsy
a neurological condition in which a person may lose consciousness and/or have convulsions

gene
any of several thousand structures on a chromosome that directs how an organism shall be formed

glaucoma
a disease in which abnormal pressure builds up within the eye

Individuals with Disabilities Education Act (IDEA)
a law passed in 1975 that ensures children with disabilities the right to public education in "the least restrictive setting possible"

mainstreaming
the practice of educating children with disabilities in regular classrooms along with nondisabled students

manic-depressive illness
a condition characterized by severe mood swings

mental retardation
a condition in which a person has a limited capacity to learn and/or to understand his or her environment

multiple sclerosis (MS)
a progressive disease of the nervous system that may cause numbness, vision loss, and paralysis

muscular dystrophy
a hereditary disease that gradually destroys the body's muscle tissue, causing progressive weakness

neurological
pertaining to the nervous system, which governs sensation and movement

paraplegia
a condition in which a person lacks movement and/or sensation in the lower portion of the body

polio (or poliomyelitis)
a viral disease that attacks the body's muscles and can cause lifelong weakness or paralysis; polio can now be prevented with a vaccine

progressive disease
any disease that grows gradually more severe over a long period of time

prosthesis
an artificial replacement for any missing part of the body (such as a limb)

quadriplegia
a condition in which a person lacks most movement and/or sensation in both the lower and upper portions of the body (below the neck)

rehabilitation
the process of training a disabled person to perform daily activities and enter the workforce

residential school
a school where students live on campus; the term usually refers to a state-run school for children with disabilities such as blindness or deafness

resource room
a special class for children with disabilities that is set up within a regular school

Section 504
a clause in the Rehabilitation Act of 1973 prohibiting discrimination against people with disabilities in any program that receives federal funds

spina bifida
a congenital condition resulting in a malformation of the spinal cord

telethon
a televised fund-raising event for a charity in which viewers pledge donations by telephone

vaccine
an injection that prevents a person from getting a disease

virus
a disease-causing agent that lives within the cells of plants, animals, and humans

To Find Out More

Books by and about the People in This Book

Anderson, Kelly. *Thomas Edison*. San Diego: Lucent Books, 1994.

Bedik, Shelley. *Thomas Edison: Great American Inventor*. New York: Scholastic, 1995.

Behrens, June. *Juliette Low: Founder of the Girl Scouts of America*. Chicago: Childrens Press, 1988.

Bentley, Judith. *Harriet Tubman*. New York: Franklin Watts, 1990.

Brown, Christy. *My Left Foot*. New York: Simon and Schuster, 1955.

Burke, Chris, and Jo-Beth McDaniel. *A Special Kind of Hero: Chris Burke's Own Story*. New York: Doubleday, 1991.

Butler, Beverly. *Gift of Gold*. New York: Pocket, 1973.
—*Light a Single Candle*. New York: Pocket, 1970.
—*Maggie by My Side*. New York: Putnam, 1988.

Callahan, John. *Don't Worry, He Won't Get Far on Foot: The Autobiography of a Dangerous Man*. New York: Vintage Books, 1990.

Campanella, Roy. *Good to Be Alive*. Lincoln, NE: University of Nebraska Press, 1995.

Duke, Patty, and Gloria Hochman. *A Brilliant Madness: Living with Manic Depressive Illness*. New York: Bantam, 1993.

Fergusson, Kitty. *Stephen Hawking: A Quest for a Theory of Everything*. New York: Bantam, 1992.

Fraser, Nancy. *Frida Kahlo: Mysterious Painter*. Woodbridge, CT: Blackbirch Press, 1992.

Freedman, Russell. *Franklin Delano Roosevelt*. New York: Clarion Books, 1990.

Gaines, Anne. *John Wesley Powell and Great Surveys of the American West.* New York: Chelsea House, 1991.

Garza, Hedda. *Frida Kahlo.* New York: Chelsea House, 1994.

Grandin, Temple, and Margaret Scariano. *Emergence: Labeled Autistic.* Novato, CA: Arena Press, 1986.

Gwaltney, John Langston. *The Dissenters: Voices from Contemporary America.* New York: Random House, 1986.

Hockenberry, John. *Moving Violations: Wheelchairs, War Zones, and Declarations of Independence.* New York: Hyperion, 1995.

Henderson, Harry. *Stephen Hawking.* San Diego: Lucent Books, 1995.

Hobbs, Mary. *The Young Milton.* New York: Roy Publishers, 1968.

Kudlinski, Kathleen V. *Juliette Gordon Low: America's First Girl Scout.* New York: Penguin, 1988.

Keeler, Stephen. *Louis Braille.* New York: Bookwright, 1986.

Keller, Helen. *The Story of My Life.* New York: Dell, 1978.

Kisor, Henry. *What's That Pig Outdoors? A Memoir of Deafness.* Boston: G. K. Hall, 1991.

Lowen, Nancy. *Beethoven.* Vero Beach, FL: Rourke, 1989.

Mankiller, Wilma, with Michael Wallis. *Mankiller.* New York: St. Martin's, 1994.

McDaniel, Melissa. *Stephen Hawking.* New York: Chelsea House, 1994.

Meltzer, Milton. *Dorothea Lange: Life Through the Camera.* New York: Puffin Books, 1986.

Nirgiotis, Nicholas. *Thomas Edison.* Chicago: Childrens Press, 1994.

Rousso, Harilyn, with Susan G. O'Malley and Mary Severance. *Disabled, Female, and Proud: Stories of Ten Women with Disabilities.* New York: Exceptional Parent Press, 1987.

Russell, Harold, with Dan Farullo. *The Best Years of My Life.* Middlebury, VT: P. S. Eriksson, 1981.

Shultz, Gladys Denny, and Daisy Gordon Lawrence. *Lady from Savannah: The Life of Juliette Low*. New York: Girl Scouts of the U.S.A., 1988.

Thompson, Wendy. *Ludwig van Beethoven*. New York: Viking Penguin, 1991.

Veeck, Bill, with Ed Linn. *Veeck—As in Wreck*. Evanston, IL: Holtzman Press, 1992.

Zonderman, John. *Helen Keller and Annie Sullivan, Working Miracles Together.* Woodbridge, CT: Blackbirch Press, 1994.

Books about the Experience of Disability

Carrillo, Anne C., Catherine Corbett, and Victoria Lewis. *No More Stares*. Berkeley, CA: Disability Rights Education and Defense Fund, 1982.
(first-person experiences of disabled women and girls)

Cheney, Glenn Allen. *Teens with Physical Disabilities: Real Life Stories of Meeting the Challenges*. Springfield, NJ: Enslow, 1995.

Driedger, Diane. *The Last Civil Rights Movement*. Los Angeles: Hearst, 1989.

Exley, Helen, ed. *What It's Like to Be Me*. New York: Friendship Press, 1984.
(children with disabilities describe their lives in words and pictures)

Feingold, S. Norman, and Norma Miller. *Your Future: A Guide for the Handicapped Teenager*. New York: R. Rosen, 1981.

Gannon, Jack R. *The Week the World Heard Gallaudet*. Washington, DC: Gallaudet University Press, 1989.

Green, Laura. *Sign-Me-Fine: Experiencing American Sign Language*. Washington, DC: Kendall Green Publishers, 1990.

Haskins, James. *Who Are the Handicapped?* Garden City, NY: Doubleday, 1978.

Haskins, James, and J. M. Stifle. *The Quiet Revolution: The Struggle for the Rights of Disabled Americans*. New York: Crowell, 1979.

Jernigan, Kenneth, ed. *The Kernel Book Series*. Baltimore, MD: National Federation of the Blind.
(collections of personal essays about the experience of blindness)

Johnson, Angela. *Humming Whispers*. New York: Orchard Books, 1995. (fiction/psychiatric illness)

Kent, Deborah. *Belonging*. New York: Dial, 1978. (fiction/blindness) —*The Disability Rights Movement*. Danbury, CT: Children's Press, 1996.

Kingsley, Jason, and Michael Levits. *Count Us In: Growing up with Down Syndrome*. New York: Harcourt Brace, 1993.

Krementz, Jill. *I Know How It Feels to Fight for Your Life*. Boston: Little, Brown, 1989. (first-person accounts of children and teens with chronic illnesses)

Kriegsman, K. H., Eleanor L. Zaslow, and Jennifer d'Zmura-Rechsteiner. *Taking Charge: Teenagers Talk about Life and Physical Disabilities*. Rockville, MD: Woodbine House, 1992.

Lang, Harry G. *Silence of the Spheres: The Deaf Experience in the History of Science*. Westport, CT: Bergin and Garvey, 1994.

Mitchell, Joyce Slayton. *See Me More Clearly: Career and Life Planning for Teens with Physical Disabilities*. New York: Harcourt Brace, 1980.

Nardo, Dawn. *The Physically Challenged*. New York: Chelsea House, 1994.

Roy, Ron. *Move Over, Wheelchairs Coming Through! Seven Young People in Wheelchairs Talk about Their Lives*. New York: Clarion Books, 1985.

Sirof, Harriet. *The Road Back: Living with a Physical Disability*. New York: New Discovery, 1993.

Slepian, Jan. *The Alfred Summer*. New York: Scholastic, 1982. (fiction/cerebral palsy, mental retardation)

Sterner, S. Philips. *Able Scientists, Disabled Persons: Biographical Sketches Illustrating Careers in the Sciences for Able Disabled Students*. Oakbrook, IL: J. Racila Associates, 1984.

Walker, LouAnn. *Hand, Heart, and Mind: The Story of the Education of America's Deaf People*. New York: Dial, 1994.

Westridge Young Writers Workshop. *Kids Explore the Gifts of Children with Special Needs*. Santa Fe: John Muir Publications, 1994. (written by the classmates of children with disabilities)

Zola, Irving Kenneth, ed. *Ordinary Lives: Voices of Disability and Disease.* Cambridge, MA: Applewood Books, 1982.

Magazines and Journals

Accent on Living, Cheever Publications, P.O. Box 700, Bloomington, IL 61702
(articles directed to people who use wheelchairs)

Common Journeys, P.O. Box 17003, Minneapolis, MN 55471
(information and support for people with chronic illness and pain)

Deaf Life, MSM Productions, 1095 Meigs Street, Rochester, NY 14620
716-328-6720 (fax)

Dialogue: A World of Ideas for Visually Impaired People of All Ages, Blindskills Inc., P.O. Box 5181, Salem, OR 97304
800-860-4224

The Disability Rag and Resource, The Advocado Press, P.O. Box 145, Louisville, KY 40201-0145
502-459-5343
(articles from the perspective of the disability rights movement)

Exceptional Parent Magazine, 209 Harvard Street, Brookline, MA 02146
617-730-5800
(articles directed toward the parents of children with disabilities)

Families, Developmental Disabilities Council, CN700, Trenton, NJ 08625
609-292-3745
(articles and interviews about families in which one or more members have a disability)

Kaleidoscope International Magazine of Literature, Fine Arts, and Disability, 326 Locust Street, Akron, OH 44302
(a literary magazine that publishes the works of people with disabilities)

Mainstream Magazine, Exploding Myths, Inc., 2973 Beach Street, San Diego, CA 92102-1529
619-234-3138
(articles and interviews featuring people with disabilities)

New Mobility, 23815 Stuart Ranch Road, Malibu, CA 90265
800-543-4116
(articles and information of special interest to people with mobility impairments)

One Step Ahead, The Disability Resource, EKA Communications, Inc., 9151 Hampton
Overlook, Capitol Heights, MD 20743
(short articles on disability-related topics)

On Our Own: A Magazine by and for Adults with Developmental and Other Disabilties, 621
Harvard Street, Brookline, MA 02146

People with Disabilities, Developmental Disabilities Council, CN700, Trenton, NJ 08625
609-292-3755
(articles focusing on current topics affecting people with disabilities)

Resourceful Woman, Health Resource Center for Women with Disabilities, 345 E.
Superior, Chicago, IL 60611
312-908-7997
(material of particular interest to women with disabilities)

Organizations and Internet Sites for and of People with Disabilities

Abledata
8455 Coleville Road, Suite 935, Silver Spring, MD 20910
800-246-2732
gopher://val-dor.cc.buffalo.edu/11/.naric/.abledata
(maintains an extensive database on technology that can enhance the lives of people with
disabilities)

ADAPT
P.O. Box 9598, Denver, CO 80209
303-333-6698
(politically active organization working to secure for people with disabilities the right to
live in their own homes with the help of personal-care assistants)

American Academy of Allergy Asthma and Immunology
11 E. Wells Street, Milwaukee, WI 53202
414-272-6071
http://excepc.com/~edi/aaaai.html

(provides publications explaining asthma and other allergies in children and adults; offers referrals to physicians around the United States)

American Cancer Society
1599 Clifton Road NE, Atlanta, GA 30329
404-320-3333
http://www.cancer.org/
(website for organization that researches symptoms, treatment, and prevention of cancer and maintains statistics regarding cancer)

American Foundation for the Blind
11 Penn Plaza, Suite 300, New York, NY 10001
800-829-0500
e-mail: afbinfo@afb.org
http://www.afb.org.afb/
(conducts research on blindness-related issues; publishes educational materials about blindness; maintains a database on blind people employed in a wide variety of occupations)

American Medical Center Cancer Information Line
1600 Pierce Street, Lakewood, CO 80214
800-525-3777
http://www.cancer.org
(provides information on all aspects of cancer; offers counseling to people with cancer and their families)

Americans with Disabilities Act Document Center
http://janweb.icdi.wvu.edu/kinder/
(contains copies of the Americans with Disabilities Act (ADA) of 1990, ADA regulations, technical assistance manuals, and many links to other disability-related websites and resources)

Arthritis Foundation
1314 Spring Street NW, Atlanta, GA 30309
800-283-7800
http://www.arthritis.org/
(organization whose mission is to find the cure for and prevention of arthritis, and to improve the quality of life for those affected by arthritis)

Autism Society of America

7910 Woodmont Avenue, Suite 650, Bethesda, MD 20814

800-328-8476

http://www.autism-society.org/

(promotes research into the causes and treatment of autism; provides publications and other information; makes referrals to local chapters that provide education and support to people with autism and their families)

Canadian Cancer Society

http://www.cancer.org/

(organization of volunteers whose mission is the eradication of cancer and the enhancement of the quality of life of people living with cancer)

Canadian Special Olympics

http://www.inconctext.ca/cso/index/html

Candlelighters Childhood Cancer Foundation

7910 Woodmont Avenue, Suite 460, Bethesda, MD 20814

800-366-2223

http://www.mindspring.com/~sonup/candlers.html

(provides information on childhood cancer; makes referrals to local support groups throughout the United States)

Center for Independent Living (CIL)

2539 Telegraph Avenue, Berkeley, CA 94704

510-841-4776 (voice); 510-841-3101 (TDD); 510-841-6168 (FAX)

http://www.ci.berkeley.ca.us/agc-cil.html

(national organization that helps people with disabilities live independently and become productive, fully participating members of society)

Centre for Neuro Skills

http://www.neuroskills.com/ncns

(website with information provided by one of the oldest and most respected brain injury rehabilitation facilities in the United States)

CF-WEB

http://www.ai.mit.edu/people/mernst/cf/

(website that provides extensive information about cystic fibrosis, including publications, lists of doctors, researchers, and support groups)

Deaf World Web

http://deafworldweb.org/deafworld/

disABILITY Information and Resources

http://www.eskimo.com/~jlubin/disabled.html

(extensive database of information about virtually every type of disability, including hundreds of links to other useful Internet sites)

Disability Rights Education and Defense Fund (DREDF)

2212 Sixth Street, Berkeley, CA 94710

510-644-2555

(leads legislative efforts on behalf of people with disabilities; advocates for disabled children and youth on educational issues)

Disabled People's International

101-7 Evergreen Place, Winnipeg, Manitoba R3L 2T3, Canada

204-287-8010 (voice); 204-284-2598 (TDD); 204-453-1364 (fax)

http://www.escape.ca/~dpi/

(brings together organizations of people with disabilities from countries around the world; encourages exchange of information and ideas to improve opportunities for disabled people worldwide)

Epilepsy Foundation of America

4351 Garden City Drive, Landover, MD 20785

800-332-1000

http://www.efa.org/

(provides information about epilepsy; offers referrals to physicians and counselors for people with epilepsy and their families)

Family Empowerment Network

http://www.downsyndrom.com/

(stories from people with Down syndrome and from their families; includes links to Internet sites concerning Down syndrome and other disabilities)

Family Village: A Global Community of Disability-Related Resources

http://www.familyvillage.wisc.edu

(website that provides information, resources, and Internet links for people around the world with disabilities, for their families, and for those who provide them with services and supports)

Gallaudet University

http://www.gallaudet.edu/

Global Child Health News & Review

http://edie/cprost/sfu.ca/gcnet/gchnr.html

(online magazine covering a wide range of issues about pediatrics and children's health)

Goodwill Industries International Inc.

http://www.goodwill.org/index.html

(organization that provides job training and employment services to millions of people with disabilities and other barriers to employment)

Helen Keller National Center

111 Middle Neck Road, Sands Point, NY 11050

(provides information on deaf-blindness; offers training in daily living skills to deaf-blind adults)

Juvenile Diabetes Foundation International/The Diabetes Research Foundation

120 Wall Street, New York, NY 10005

800-JDF-CURE

http://www/jdfcure.com/

(a not-for-profit, voluntary health agency whose mission is to support and fund research to find a cure for diabetes and its complications; website includes information on local JDF chapters, diabetes research, and the JDF Walk for the Cure)

Muscular Dystrophy Association

National Headquarters, 3300 East Sunrise Drive, Tucson, AZ 85718

http://www.mdausa.org

(worldwide organization committed to researching neuromuscular disorders and assisting people living with such disorders)

National Association of the Deaf

814 Thayer Avenue, Silver Spring, MD 20910

301-587-1788

(provides information about deafness; advocates for the rights of deaf people)

National Council on Independent Living

2111 Wilson Boulevard, Arlington, VA 22201

703-525-3406 (voice); 703-525-3407 (TDD); 703-525-3408 (fax)

(represents centers for independent living throughout the United States; works to pass legislation to increase opportunities for people with disabilities)

National Down Syndrome Congress
1605 Chantilly Drive, Suite 250, Atlanta, GA 30324
800-232-NDSC
e-mail: ndsc@chartiesusa.com
http://www.carol.net/~ndsc

National Down Syndrome Society
666 Broadway, New York, NY 10012
800-221-4602; 212-460-9330
(provides publications and other information conveying a positive attitude toward people with Down syndrome; makes referrals to local chapters throughout the country)

National Easter Seal Foundation
5120 S. Hyde Park Boulevard, Chicago, IL 60615
312-726-6200
(provides physical therapy and other services to children with disabilities)

National Empowerment Center
20 Ballard Road, Lawrence, MA 01843
800-769-3728 (800-POWER2U)
(provides information about organizations of and for psychiatric survivors; helps to start local programs around the country)

National Federation of the Blind
1800 Johnson Street, Baltimore, MD 21230
410-659-9317
(provides publications and other information conveying positive attitudes about blindness; advocates for the rights of blind people of all ages; offers referrals to chapters throughout the United States)

National Foundation for Depressive Illness
P.O. Box 2257, New York, NY 10116
800-248-4344
(provides information about depressive and manic-depressive illness; offers referral to physicians and counselors)

National Information Center for Children and Youth with Disabilities
P.O. Box 1492, Washington, DC 20013
800-695-0285
(maintains a database on organizations throughout the United States that serve young
people with disabilities)

National Multiple Sclerosis Society
733 Third Avenue, New York, NY 10017
http://www.nmss.org/
(extensive information about multiple sclerosis, treatment, research, and local MS chapters)

National Parkinson Foundation
1501 NW Ninth Avenue, Miami, FL 33136
http://www.parkinson.org
(news about Parkinson's disease, readings, and notices of conferences)

National Rehabilitation Information Center (NARIC)
8455 Colesville Road, Suite 935, Silver Spring, MD 20910
800-346-2742 (voice); 301-587-1967 (fax); 301-589-1967 (BBS)
http://www.naric.com/naric
(a 46,000-volume library and information center on disability and rehabilitation)

National Spinal Cord Injury Hotline
2201 Argonne Drive, Baltimore, MD 21218
800-526-3456
(provides information about spinal cord injury; makes referrals to peer counseling groups
throughout the United States)

Office on Americans with Disabilities Act
Civil Rights Division, U.S. Department of Justice, P.O. Box 66118, Washington, DC 20035
202-614-0301 (voice); 202-514-0380 or -0381 (TDD); 202-514-6193 (BBS)
(explains the rights of people with disabilities under the law; handles discrimination
complaints filed under the ADA)

Our Kids
http://wonder.mit.edu/ok
(website aimed at providing medical and research information, resources, Internet links,
and reading lists to parents of children with special needs)

Special Olympics International
1325 G Street NW, Suite 500, Washington, DC 20005
202-628-3630
http://www.specialolympics.org/
(sponsors training and competition in a variety of sports for people with mental retardation)

Spina Bifida Association of America
4590 MacArthur Boulevard NW, Suite 250, Washington, DC 20007
800-621-3141
(provides information on spina bifida; makes referrals to local support groups for people with spina bifida and their families)

Telecommunications for the Deaf, Inc.
8719 Colesville Road, Suite 300, Silver Spring, MD 20910
301-589-3786 (voice); 301-589-3006 (TDD)
(provides information on relay systems and adaptive devices that enable deaf persons to use the telephone)

Trace Research and Development Center on Communication, Control, and Computer Access for Handicapped Individuals
5151 Waisman Center, University of Wisconsin-Madison, 1500 Highland Avenue, Madison, WI 53705
608-262-6966
(develops technology for severely disabled persons who have speech difficulties; provides information about available communication devices)

Traumatic Brain Injury & Epilepsy Links
http://canddwilson.com/tbi/tbiepil/htm
(includes information, first-person stories, poems about traumatic brain injury and adult seizure disorders; provides links to other organizations as well as to numerous personal home pages)

U.S. Association of Blind Athletes
31 North Institute Drive, Colorado Springs, CO 80903
719-630-0422
(sponsors training and competition for blind athletes in a variety of sports)

United Cerebral Palsy Association
1522 K Street NW, Suite 1112, Washington, DC 20005
202-842-1266
http://www.ucpa.org/
(provides information and publications about cerebral palsy; makes referrals to local chapters that provide education and support services)

U.S. Cerebral Palsy Athletic Association
200 Harrison Avenue, Newport, RI 02840
401-848-2460
http://uscpaa.org/
(sponsors training and competition in a variety of sports for athletes with cerebral palsy)

Wheelchair Access & News
http://www.inet-usa.com/wca/
(includes sales information about wheelchair-accessible homes, vans, cars, and restaurants, as well as extensive links to numerous areas of interest to people with disabilities)

Wheelchair Sports USA
3595 East Fountain Boulevard, Suite L-1, Colorado Springs, CO 80910
(sponsors training and competition throughout the country for athletes who use wheelchairs)

World Institute on Disability
510 Sixteenth Street, Suite 100, Oakland, CA 94612
510-763-4100 (voice); 510-763-4109 (fax); 510-208-9493 (TDD)
(sponsors research on issues related to disability; provides information on disability to policymakers and interested individuals)

Selected Internet Newsgroups on Disability Issues

arthritis	alt.support.arthritis
	misc.health.arthritis
asthma	alt.support.asthma
autism	bit.listserv.autism
blindness	alt.comp.blind-users
	bitlistserv.blindnws
cancer	alt.support.cancer
	sci.med.diseases.cancer

cerebral palsy	alt.support.cerebral-palsy
cystic fibrosis	sci.med.cysticfibrosis
deafness	bit.listserv.deaf-l
diabetes	alt.support.diabetes.kids
	misc.health.diabetes
Down syndrome	bit.listserv.down-syn
eating disorders	alt.support.eating-disor
epilepsy	alt.support.epilepsy
learning disabilties	alt.support.learning-disab
multiple sclerosis	alt.support.mult-sclerosis
muscular dystrophy	alt.support.musc-dystrophy
polio/post-polio	alt.support.post-polio
schizophrenia	alt.support.schizophrenia
spina bifida	alt.support.spina-bifida

INDEX

About the Authors

Deborah Kent grew up in Little Falls, New Jersey, where she was the first blind student to attend the local public school. She received a B.A. in English from Oberlin College in 1969. In 1971, she earned a master's degree from Smith College School for Social Work. When she began seeking a job in her field, many employers told her that they would not hire her because of her blindness. At last, she turned for help to the American Civil Liberties Union (ACLU). The ACLU explained that existing laws did not protect people with disabilities from discrimination. If she wanted help, she would first have to change the law.

After a long job search, Ms. Kent found a social work position at the University Settlement House in New York City. While living in New York, she joined the National Federation of the Blind (NFB), an organization of blind persons working to fight discrimination. In 1973, the NFB helped to obtain protection for people with disabilities under the New York State Human Rights Act. Ms. Kent was thrilled by the chance to work with other disabled people for a common cause. Just as the ACLU had suggested, she worked to help change the law.

After four years as a social worker, Ms. Kent decided to try her hand at writing. She moved to San Miguel de Allende in Mexico, a town with a thriving community of foreign writers and artists. Drawing upon her experiences as a blind student in a regular high school, she wrote her first young-adult novel, *Belonging*. In San Miguel, she also helped to start the Centro de Crecimiento, a school for children with disabilities.

Ms. Kent is the author of more than a dozen young-adult novels, as well as numerous children's nonfiction books published by Children's Press and other publishers. She remains an active member of the National Federation of the Blind and lives in Chicago with her husband, children's author R. Conrad Stein, and their daughter, Janna.

Kathryn A. Quinlan was born in Bloomington, Minnesota, and moved to Illinois during her early teens. In 1982, she received a B.A. in English and philosophy from Augustana College. She then moved to Chicago, where she worked in publishing for several years. During this time, she also served as a personal-care attendant for a college student with a disability. This experience increased her awareness of the need for accessible buildings and public transportation, as well as for equal educational and professional opportunities for people with disabilities.

Ms. Quinlan is now a marketing and communications professional for a large insurance and consulting services corporation. She and her husband, Denis J. Quinlan, live in Chicago and volunteer for the Chicago branch of Recording for the Blind and Dyslexic, an organization that records textbooks for individuals with reading-related disabilities.